WAR MACHINES
SEA

WAR MACHINES
SEA

Edited by TOM PERLMUTTER

Octopus Books

Introduction

Within the terms of this book, a formidable war machine is a machine (or even a technique) that gives its possessor an edge over the enemy. At sea, for example, the introduction of the stern rudder was a major breakthrough which transformed the oared longship into the sailing man-o'-war. The development of broadside fire power by England's Henry VIII was another momentous breakthrough. The introduction of steam in the 19th Century, the replacement of wood by iron plates, the major milestone of the revolving gun turret — all these adaptations of inventive technology gave the nations that first practised them a technical supremacy in weaponry. The rise and fall of civilisation and of power groupings is very largely a reflection of a nation's prowess in technology and of its skill in adapting that technology to the needs of war.

This book is a selection of the most memorable development points in the machinery or 'mechanics' of sea warfare. It begins with the Pharaohs and ends with Polaris — although the story, like human inventiveness, really has no end.

In a sense this book is a pictorial catalogue which — with its companion volumes on machines of land and air warfare — helps the reader to build up a 'time-scale' picture of the ebb and flow of civilisations and of the gradual growth of that background technology which now dominates every aspect of our lives.

Top: The Royal Navy's battleship Thunderer. *Below: The German U-35 with its fluttering pennants proclaiming its victims.*

Contents

First published in 1975 by
Octopus Books Limited
59 Grosvenor Street
London W1
under licence from
Lynx Press Ltd.
601 Union House
Hong Kong

Created and devised by
Berkeley Publishers Ltd.

ISBN 0 7064 0415 7

© 1975 Lynx Press Ltd.

Distributed in USA by
Crescent Books
a division of
Crown Publishers Inc.
419 Park Avenue South
New York NY 10016

Printed in Hong Kong

An Egyptian papyrus boat used on the River Nile, c.3000 B.C.

WAR AT SEA

THE EARLY SEAFARERS

At Medinet Habu, in the tomb of Egypt's last great pharaoh, Ramses III, there is a carving of a naval engagement fought between the Egyptians and the dreaded 'people from the sea'. The carving is significant for it is the first extant illustration of a naval combat. There must have been many hostile encounters on the sea prior to that battle, for wherever men gather there arise conflicts of interest. Yet no earlier ones are

The earliest surviving illustration of naval combat, from the tomb of Ramses III (c. 1200 B.C.). Shows the use of archers and spearmen.

recorded. Evidently, Ramses III's battle is the first one to impress itself on the minds of the ancients. In effect this is where the history of naval warfare begins. What were the early sea-fights like? What kind of boats were in use and how were they manned? And what were the weapons that gave final victory to Ramses?

More than two thousand years of experience went into the construction of Ramses' warships. Egyptians were river people. They depended almost completely on the Nile for their livelihood and for centuries they had built boats and sailed and paddled on the broad back of the Nile.

The earliest boats were constructed of the most readily available material – papyrus. The papyrus boats were spool-shaped with pointed prows bent upward to enable easy shore handling. They were paddled, though a rectangular mast was situated in the forward part of the craft.

It is not until much later (c.3000 B.C.) that we find illustrations of oarsmen. The exchange of paddle for oar was a major innovation, for the oar proved to be a much more flexible and controlled means of propulsion. For the next 4500 years oars were to be the main motive force for all warships until the coming of the cannon made the sail a more practicable alternative.

Egypt under the pharaohs became a richer nation and was able to import wood for its vessels. The wooden boats were built in a peculiar fashion which was to remain the norm for centuries to come. Since the Egyptians had not then come upon the idea of ribs, thick wooden blocks held

Bas-relief of Egyptian ships from the tomb of Sahu-Re, c.3000 B.C. Note the cable stretching from fore to aft, used to prevent the extremities from drooping.

together by wooden pegs were used instead. Water pressure forced the blocks together while at either end ropes were tied round the hull to strengthen the structure.

From the rivers, the Egyptians made ever widening excursions into the Mediterranean. For the longer sea voyages the boats had to be further strengthened as well as prepared to meet the forces of the hostile naval powers of Crete and Phoenicia. Thick blocks were still the basic method of construction but for additional support a strong twisted rope was stretched over several queen posts fore and aft. In addition the bipod mast was collapsible, allowing easier manoeuvrability for the oarsmen in unfavourable weather or when engaged in military action. The oarsmen stood, thus gaining greater impetus and speed. The relief carvings on the pyramids at Abu Sir also show stem and stern posts – the fore post carrying the protective, all-seeing eye of Osiris.

Around 1500 B.C. Queen Hatshepsut sent a convoy of ships to the land of Punt. The temple at Deir el Bahari has detailed relief carvings of her vessels. The general features were the same as the earlier ones but in detail the ships had improved. The hulls were constructed around a high and strong keel-plank which projected up and inward in the aft while projecting forward in the fore. The mast was moved closer to the centre and the square sail became considerably larger. Two great steering oars with tillers replaced the six small steering oars in the bow.

Three hundred years later (1200 B.C.), Ramses III built a fleet that was to defeat the invaders from the north. His ships were basically the same as those of Queen Hatshepsut yet a few important

An Egyptian sea-going vessel of about 2500 B.C. Ships like this were tougher than they may have looked. This one has just left port and is heading for the open sea. The crew are raising the mast from its support amidships, preparing to set sail.

adaptations were made, borrowings from the maritime invaders.

Interesting new features were the high washboards to protect the oarsmen; furling of sails by means of vertical brails, an advancement over the previously existing necessity of lowering the yard; and a crow's nest atop the mast. The ships were about 80 to 90 feet long and usually carried about 30 oarsmen in addition to military personnel.

The invaders, the 'northerners of the isles', were a tough sea-faring people from the Aegean Islands and the Mediterranean coast line. Driven from their own bases they moved southwards to Egypt. The relief at Medinet Habu shows the invaders in full sail, in other words unprepared for combat. For until the coming of the cannon naval combat meant hand-to-hand fighting, ramming or archery. All these manoeuvres depended on skilful oarsmanship. Sails did not allow the necessary flexibility in battle, and the ram had as yet not been invented.

Quite rightly, since it was the Egyptians who had first discovered the oar (*c.*3000 B.C.), 1800 years later Ramses was able to prove his supreme skill with it in battle. Caught unawares, sails still flying, the invaders suffered a crushing defeat. Egypt was saved. Unfortunately, the death of Ramses III signalled the decline of Egypt and it is to the rude maritime peoples of the north that we must look for further developments in warships.

THE PENTEKONTER AND THE POWER OF THE RAM

For several centuries (about 1100 B.C. to 800 B.C.) the Phoenicians were the undoubted masters of the Mediterranean. Their ships roamed the seas from the shores of Syria to Carthage in northern Africa, to the Atlantic coast of Spain on the outskirts of the then known world, and even beyond in an aggressive search for trade and wealth.

Because they were a trading nation the Phoenicians had to develop a powerful naval fighting force to protect their trade routes. Necessity led to creative experimentation in the shipwright's craft and to the first significant improvements in ship design.

The earliest warships of the northern Mediterranean were large narrow dug-outs. The dug-outs had sharp jutting rams but these were merely extensions of the main body of the vessel and not specialized for military purposes. The dug-outs were fitted with outriggers to handle the oars.

To increase the fighting power of the vessel the Phoenicians developed the *pentekonter* – a type of bireme (i.e. a galley with two banks of oars). The basic design of the dug-out was maintained but the outriggers were planked-in allowing for an extra rank of rowers. The top thwart extended outward from the hull leaving room for the extra rank on a lower level below the raised decks. The inner oars were placed through oar ports cut out of the hull.

The pentekonter was approximately 60 feet long and carried 50 oarsmen. The ram had by now become a powerful weapon and extended from the hull into a sharp point just below water level. The mast was situated amidships and carried a large square sail. The supports of the narrow upper deck tied the thwarts to the bottom of the boat and stiffened the whole structure. At maximum efficiency the pentekonter could race at six knots.

Above: Side section of the pentekonter, showing the ram projecting forward below the water line.
Left: Outriggers provided space for a second bank of oarsmen and left room for soldiers in the centre of the vessel.

Officers and soldiers were stationed on the narrow upper deck while the rowers had their weapons ready. In battle they stayed by their oars.

The advantages of the new design were many. The narrow, easily propelled hull of the dug-out was maintained; a narrow deck for soldiers and archers was added without upsetting the efficiency of the oarsmen or the balance of the vessel; and, finally, with the addition of an extra rank of rowers, the vessel moved at a greater speed enabling a much more powerful ramming force.

The pentekonter, undoubtedly, proved its worth many times in maintaining Phoenician supremacy on the sea for such a long period. And even when Phoenician power was on the decline, challenged by the young, upstart city states of Greece, the pentekonter proved itself a weapon to be feared.

An early bas-relief of a Phoenician pentekonter. These were the ships that established the Phoenician empire.

The Battle of Alalia

The Phocaeans were the first of the Greeks to perform long voyages and to establish colonies in the western Mediterranean, in what was once the sole preserve of the Phoenicians. But not only did they set up colonies, they also began to harrass their neighbours and indulge in piracy. This the Phoenicians would not stand.

Together with their Etruscan allies they gathered 60 men of war and sailed to Alalia in Corsica where the Phocaeans had their headquarters. Though the Phocaeans had also mustered 60 ships they were no match for the Phoenicians, whose ships, fitted with bronze and wooden rams, demolished the Phocaean fleet in a matter of hours. Two-thirds of their fleet was destroyed and the rest had their rams so badly wrenched as to make them unfit for service. The Battle of Alalia was important in two respects. First, it prevented the Mediterranean from becoming a Greek lake; and second, it determined the nature of naval warfare to come. The role of the ram was thenceforth established. The first move had been taken to distinguish naval tactics from land tactics. No longer was a preponderance of soldiers and archers necessary for victory. Victory depended more on the speed and sturdiness of the vessel and the skill of the oarsmen and captain to manoeuvre the ship properly in battle.

THE TRIREME RULES THE SEA

The Greeks were quick to learn from the Phoenicians and they soon developed their own biremes which further advanced the shipwright's art.

The bireme was more than just an extension of the dug-out; it was a ribbed ship with a proper keel and a carvel-built hull which provided stability and strength in the face of enemy ramming.

The two hundred years from 500 B.C. to 300 B.C. constituted the classical age of Greek shipping, which saw the development of some of the most graceful ships ever known, ships that were light, sturdy and elegant of line. And the prince of the classical ships was the trireme.

No other ship has caused as much difficulty in

interpretation as the trireme. Like the bireme, it was born out of a desire to create a faster ship which would not lose anything in lightness, manoeuvrability or sturdiness. The faster the ship the greater ramming power it possessed and speed depended on the number of oarsmen that could be fitted into a vessel. The problem was, therefore, to add another bank of rowers on to existing vessels without making them cumbersome.

There are a few generally accepted facts about the trireme. We know that its maximum length was 135 feet with a beam of about 20 feet; that it lay low in the water with eight feet of freeboard above the waterline and a draught of approximately three feet. We also know that it had a crew of around 200, including 170 oarsmen known as *thalamites* (27 to a side), *zeugites* (27) and *thranites* (31). The remaining crew were made up of officers and military personnel, which usually included foot-soldiers and archers.

There was little storage room on the trireme, which meant that it had to be close to land bases to restock on supplies. The mast, situated amidships, was, was lowered in time of battle.

The whole ship was considered as a weapon and eventually the ram became a separate, detachable instrument which could be replaced when necessary. The early triremes were incompletely decked and the top row of oarsmen would be protected by the shields of soldiers placed on the outrigger. Difficulties in interpretation arise when we look at the actual seating of the oarsmen. There are two main theories which try to resolve the question, both nautically sound but there is little direct evidence for the first.

This theory holds that the thwarts were placed at an oblique angle running from the centre line of the ship forward and outward. Two oarsmen (the outermost were the thranites, the ones nearest to the centre-line the zeugites) sat side by side on the upper thwart and had their oars running through ports on the outrigger. The third oarsman (the thalamite) would swing his oar between the upper two and have it run through a port in the hull just above the water-line.

The second, and more likely, theory states that the oarsmen were in three rows one above the other, the oarsman above seated a little forward of the one below him.

Far Left: Three ranks of oarsmen gave additional speed to the trireme but created seating problems. Below: A trireme of the 4th Century B.C., with a fearsome ram, two stern rudders and a sail full set. Triremes were responsible for the Greek's stirring victory against the invading Persian fleet at Salamis.

THE FORMIDABLE FIRE–SHIP

Even the victory against the Persians at Salamis, where the trireme triumphed, could not stop the Greek city-states from quarrelling amongst themselves; a quarrel which finally erupted into the thirty years long Peloponnesian War, a war which doomed Greece's fragile independence. To the west, however, a new world power was slowly gathering strength. That power was Rome.

The Romans were quick to learn the art of shipbuilding as they spread across, first the Italian peninsula, and then, further afield, the Mediterranean. Rome came to depend on its ships for its daily bread and for the transport of troops to protect its far-flung empire.

Their first ships were biremes and triremes on the Greek model. But the Roman taste for size soon asserted itself; the triremes became quinqueremes and septiremes – that is, vessels with five or seven banks of oarsmen. The deck became completely covered and a fighting tower was erected in the stern. These ships were formidable indeed yet curiously enough it was not the quinquereme or the septireme but the lowly fire-ship which decided the fate of the Empire.

A fire-ship is an old, unmanned ship filled with combustible materials. In combat it is set alight and directed at the enemy fleet in the hope of setting it on fire. Wooden ships were very vulnerable to that sort of tactic and fire-ships, if used effectively, could be deadly. They had never been used so effectively before as at the Battle of Actium (31 B.C.).

Right: A Roman warship. This trireme has a double steering paddle, one on each side. There is a fighting tower at the front, soldiers on the deck and a small but highly effective ram at the prow. Above: Another example of a Roman warship.

Marc Antony's Defeat at Actium

Actium is the promontory on the south side of the entrance to the Gulf of Ambracia (today Arta) in northwestern Greece. In ancient times Actium was situated in unhealthy marshland that harboured disease-carrying insects. It was at Actium in 32 B.C. that Marc Antony set up a base camp preparatory to an attack on Italy.

Ever since the assassination of Julius Caesar the Roman Republic had been beset by factional strife and civil war. Thirteen years later only two contestants were left in the arena – Octavian, Caesar's grand-nephew and designated heir, and Marc Antony, Caesar's lieutenant. With the aid of Cleopatra and the wealth of Egypt Antony had set up a powerful mini-kingdom in the east. But it was Rome that he wanted.

Antony's main supply lines lay along the Peloponnesian coast stretching from Patras in the north to Methane in the south-west, to Corinth and from there by sea to Egypt and Asia. The supply line was as vital to Antony as, four and a half centuries earlier, it had been to the Persians – Greece was still much too poor a country to support a large invading force.

While Antony gathered troops and material and waited for an auspicious time for the crossing, Agrippa, Octavian's naval commander and a brilliant tactician, massed his fleet of small, light and very fast ships at Brindisium. He quickly crossed the Adriatic, setting up a post north of Antony's. Instead of offering battle immediately Agrippa shrewdly began to erode Antony's supply routes. One by one Antony's garrisons fell – Methane, Patras and finally Corinth. Agrippa occupied the island of Leucas, just south of the Gulf of Ambracia, a base closer to the enemy.

Antony's army, hungry, ill and demoralized, began to fall apart. The number of desertions

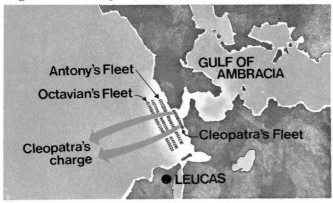

Antony and Cleopatra escaped but lost at Actium

increased daily. Antony had to act soon or he would have had no army left to fight with, much less conquer an empire. It was necessary to put aside his dream of taking Rome in the interests of survival. He had to find some way back to Egypt and comparative safety. Once back he could refurbish his forces and set out anew, wiser and more wary of his cunning foe. But first – how to get back? The overland route was too hazardous and, besides, would take much too long. His only choice was to break Agrippa's sea blockade. On September 2, 31 B.C., Antony readied his fleet for battle and flight, a fleet which was composed of the large and somewhat cumbersome quinqueremes and septiremes, which, to add to their awkwardness, had timber structures fitted to the hulls as anti-ramming devices.

As the morning progressed the fleets drew into position. The forces of Octavian lay in wait at the entrance to the Gulf. Octavian held the honoured right flank, Agrippa the left, where he could expect to face Antony.

Antony's force issued forth slowly, cautiously

hugging the shore line. A squadron of 60 Egyptian warships under Cleopatra's command kept to the rear. Antony moved from ship to ship giving orders and encouraging his men. He ordered them to stay put and wait for the enemy to move first. But the enemy refused to act. Agrippa had patience and plenty of time. If the battle was not joined today then it would be tomorrow. Each day would see a further attrition of morale in the camp of Marc Antony.

The day dragged. Marc Antony grew nervous and impatient with the waiting. At last, unable to restrain himself any longer, he gave the signal to attack. The left wing opened by advancing towards the enemy. Agrippa countered by moving northward to entice Antony's ships to move forward and apart from each other. The stratagem worked and Agrippa's faster ships were able to converge in lightning attacks on Antony's solitary vessels. Swiftly moving in and out, Agrippa's ships caused havoc by ramming or, more frequently, by stripping the enemy's oars which were too heavy to be shipped quickly. Even so no rout was to be had. Antony's ships

were cumbersome but they were sturdy and his men fought hard and valiantly.

Meanwhile Cleopatra, seeing her chance, broke through both centre lines and sailed for home, followed close at heel by Antony.

Despite Antony's desertion the battle raged on as fiercely as ever. On both sides the fighting men were Romans, strongly disciplined in their trade and with similar methods of battle.

Agrippa was no usual commander, however. He earned his name by his ingenuity and his ability to apply novel methods of fighting in battle. He fought to win, not as a gentleman's game of honour. So when, at Actium, the usual methods of combat did not produce the desired result he brought out the flame throwers and the fire-ships. Catapults tossed blazing missiles (pots of flaming charcoal and pitch) at the enemy. Rafts laden with combustible materials were set alight and thrown into the ranks of Antony's fleet. By late afternoon the battle was over. Antony's forces could not stand up to this kind of assault. Antony's fate was sealed. Octavian had proved himself master of Rome.

THE DROMON – A COASTAL RUNNER

For 250 years thereafter the Mediterranean remained a Roman sea. The Roman fleet reverted to being a kind of coast guard protecting the shipping lanes and suppressing piracy wherever it arose. As the Roman Empire crumbled under the impact of barbarian invasions all attention was concentrated on beating back the Germanic and Asiatic invaders. These were essentially land affairs and little money or time or energy was left for the development of the navy.

In the east the Byzantine Empire became stabilized and revived the coast guard activities of the old Roman navy. A type of warship was evolved which became known as the *dromon*, literally 'the runner'.

Not much is known of the dromon but, as its name indicates, it was presumably a fast warship with 50 thwarts on two levels making for a total

The Dromon was a fast coastguard runner, developed by the Byzantine Empire. The lethal ram was retained, raised above the water line perhaps to give added speed and to break up the oars of the enemy vessel. With ships like these, the Byzantines defeated the Gothic invaders.

of 100 oarsmen. Later on the ship was equipped with a forecastle which was used as a fighting tower. Another interesting feature was that the ram was elevated well above the water line.

Eventually, the dromon became a general term for warships and several types developed, such as the Pamphylian Chelander – a smaller and lighter version of the earlier dromon; or the galea, which was an armed reconnaissance boat.

The Battle of Sena Gallica

The first important naval battle of the regenerated fleet took place in the reign of Justinian I (482–565). He had established peace with the Persians on his eastern frontier and was eager to reunite the Roman Empire. And over a period of 30 years his aims were achieved by two very remarkable generals – Belisarius and the Armenian eunuch, Narses.

Belisarius had done much to reconquer Italy from the Goths but Byzantine politics and the lack of adequate military back-up support, led him to resign his commission. The Goths rapidly encroached on the conquered territory and were soon at the doors of Ancona, the gateway to the Adriatic.

The Byzantines had to obtain a foothold in the Adriatic in order to ferry troops and supplies to the Italian peninsula. At Salona, on the Greek side of the Adriatic, a combined force of army and navy was being assembled. By the summer of 551 the forces only awaited the arrival of Narses to lead them on to victory.

Narses, however, was delayed in Constantinople on Imperial business and in the meanwhile the situation was growing critical on the Italian side of the peninsula. Ravenna, the last Byzantine stronghold on the peninsula, could not hold out much longer against its besiegers. Valerian, its commander, sent a desperate request to Salona for reinforcements to avert disaster.

Happily, Narses had as a subordinate an able commander who took the initiative at this crucial juncture. With 38 dromons he crossed the Adriatic and joined Valerian's fleet of 12. Together they sailed to Sena Gallica, about 17 miles northwest of Ancona.

The Gothic force of about 47 vessels hurried northwards to offer battle. The fleets faced each other – the Byzantines, with their greater experience of the sea, in an orderly and well spaced line; the novice Gothic seamen huddled together in close formation.

The Goths, pursuing their land tactics, rushed forward in a massive attack in an attempt to grapple with the enemy. But what worked on land did not work at sea. Their ships collided, a lot of time was wasted separating themselves from tangles and meanwhile the Byzantine archers, taking careful aim, picked off the Goths and rammed their ships.

The Goths were helpless. The engagement was a total defeat for them, with a loss of 36 ships.

GREEK FIRE HALTS THE SARACEN

Soon the Byzantine emperors had more pressing concerns than a distant empire in the west. A new and very dangerous enemy had arisen in the east – the Saracens. But at the same time the Byzantines developed what was undoubtedly the single most powerful weapon in the ancient world – Greek fire, and it was with Greek fire that the Saracen onslaught was stayed.

In 622 Muhammed made his famous *hegira* (or pilgrimage) to Medina and established an Islamic brotherhood of the Arabic tribes. In the years to come the Arab tribes, fired by the passion of their new religion, spread across the greater part of the then known world from Persia to the western coasts of Spain. But in their path stood a seemingly weak and degenerate Empire – Byzantium. An easy conquest, the Arabs thought. Yet over and over again the Byzantines exhibited a great resilience and inner strength. And although her territories were slowly eaten away over the years she did not finally succumb until 1453 to the steamrolling power of a rising eastern nation, the Ottoman Turks. Twice the Saracens tried to capture Constantinople, the capital and heart of the Empire, and twice they failed. Byzantine ingenuity defeated the massed attacks of the Arab navies. For when the Saracens arrived at the gates of Constantinople they were greeted by the awesome and overpowering force of Greek fire.

Greek fire was the name given to a series of incendiary compounds consisting of, in various proportions and combinations, naphtha, bitumen, pitch, sulphur, vegetable gums, resins of coniferous trees, turpentine and oil. Often quick lime was added to make 'moist fire' so called because water would greatly increase its volatility. A perfect weapon against the fire-prone wooden vessels of those days.

Greek fire placed in closed earthen pots with an attached wick would be catapulted or thrown by hand at the enemy. On ships, however, the more usual means of fire was through long copper tubes placed in the bow.

The tubes were shaped into gargoyles, horrendous masks of fabulous monsters meant to instil panic in the enemy. A pneumatic device worked the actual firing mechanism, blowing the compound through the tube where it would be lit as it emerged from the other end. A contemporary account describes how the compound would 'burst into flame and fall like a streak of lightning on the faces of the men opposite'.

It is difficult to conceive the great horror caused by the sudden unleashing of that monstrous weapon. Nothing like it had been seen before. More than 500 years after its invention John of Joinville called it 'a dragon flying through the air'.

In 900 the Emperor Leo VI, the Wise, wrote of the 'fire prepared in tubes (issuing forth) with a noise of thunder, a fiery smoke which burns the ship at which it is directed'.

The Siege of Constantinople

When the Caliph Walid died in 715 the Arabian Empire stretched from Asia to Spain. Yet the Byzantine Empire lay like a thorn in its side. The great expedition against Constantinople in 677 had ended in miserable failure with most of the retreating Moslem fleet lost in a storm. For the next 40 years or so internal disputes prevented a renewal of hostilities. Finally peace was

In the simpler form of bellows, the burning mixture was poured down the barrel and then blown quickly out again. The ladles and pot were used for pouring and brewing the fire.

In the more sophisticated bellows, the mixture was kept on the boil in the built-in pot. A valve stopped it from being sucked back into the bellows themselves.

restored in the land and in 715 Suleiman assumed the Caliphate. He was determined to humble the Byzantines.

Constantinople, the object of the Saracen attack, was a virtually impregnable fortress. It was located on a promontory flanked on the north by the Golden Horn and on the south by the Sea of Marmosa. To the west lay a strong double wall – one of the finest military fortifications of antiquity. The Imperial fleet lay in the Golden Horn protected by a chain that lay across the narrow opening to the sea.

The only way to take the city was by starving it out, which was the plan adopted by the Arabs. Suleiman appointed his brother, Moslemah, commander-in-chief of the armed forces, while Suleiman the General was to command the fleet. Victory depended on a complete blockade of Constantinople by land and sea.

On August 15, 717, Moslemah arrived before Constantinople with an army 80,000 strong.

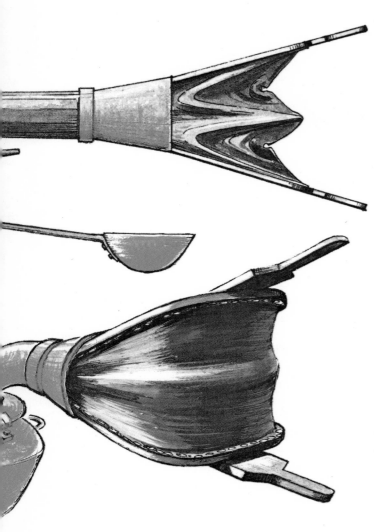

Immediately he set about digging a deep ditch round the city. However, the crucial factor lay at sea. For not only did the Saracen fleet have to supply all the necessities of the besiegers, it also had to cut off Byzantine communications both to the north and south.

Suleiman the General sailed into Byzantine waters with a fleet of 1,800 warships and fast sailers, two weeks after Moslemah had positioned his forces. The fleet was divided into two detachments: one stationed at Eutropicus on the Asiatic coast, to cut off supplies from the Aegean; the other was to move through the Bosphorous above the city and cut off communications with the Black Sea and the rich grain fields of the north.

On September 3, 717, the second squadron set sail for its objective. As it approached the Golden Horn, Leo, the Byzantine Emperor, ordered the great chain to be lowered and in a lightning attack let loose the ship-destroying Greek fire. Twenty enemy vessels were smashed before the rest of the party retreated to the safety of the Horn. The guerrilla raid proved so successful that Leo kept the boom lowered hoping thus to lure the remainder of the squadron into the narrow isthmus where it could be destroyed at leisure. Fearing a trap, the enemy declined the proposal. Constantinople remained open to her vital supplies.

The coming of winter saw the death of the caliph and of Suleiman the General. The Saracen troops were decimated by the cold and disease, yet they persisted in their folly. Further reinforcements were sent in the spring, when a squadron of 400 Egyptian ships managed to sneak into the Bosphorous, succeeding where Suleiman had failed. Constantinople faced the prospect of a slow death by starvation.

Fortunately for Leo most of the enemy crew were impressed Christian slaves and many of these deserted. They were able to provide Leo with precise details on the enemy formation. Acting quickly Leo lowered the boom and caught the Moslem fleet by surprise. The copper mouths spewed their deadly fire, the Christian crew rose up in rebellion against their masters, and soon the enemy vessels were easily subjugated. Leo had won a decisive naval victory. The back of the siege was broken. On August 15, 718, one year to the date of its inception, the siege was lifted and the Arab army retreated south in ignominy. It was a great victory for the Byzantines thanks to the destructive power of Greek fire.

THE VIKING LONGSHIP

For the next major developments in maritime warfare we must turn our attention northward where the Viking longship set new standards of ship construction. At the same time that the elaborate and sophisticated Byzantine court was fighting for its life in the semi-tropical waters of the Mediterranean there appeared in Northern Europe a fearless race of warriors who were making the sea their second home – the Vikings.

The peninsular nature of Scandanavia, her innumerable fjords, and the difficulty of access through the interior made it natural for the Vikings to take to the water. They led a harsh life governed by the strict code of the fighter. The skalds, their national epics, spoke of great contests and mighty deeds in battle. And many of the most famous battles took place on the sea.

As in other parts of the world the Viking warship, the longship, was an adaptation of existing shipping, either fishing or merchant

Gokstad ship, showing fixed rudder (without tiller).

Clinker-built and riveted this Viking ship has a

vessels. Their ships, however, differed radically from those in the Levant. Naturally so, for the challenges that the Viking shipwright had to face were of a different sort from those in the Mediterranean. The northern seas were harsher and more turbulent than those in the south. The Viking ship had to withstand greater stress, especially on the long, lone voyages across the Atlantic. Finally, the enemies they faced were fellow Vikings, not some alien power. And in battle honour was to be had by honest fighting, not by the cunning blow of the ram to the rear.

One of the earliest and most finely preserved examples of the Viking ship is the Gokstad vessel dated to the 10th Century. Not quite a longship,

it provides the prototype of the Viking warship. Seventy-nine feet long and sixteen feet across at its widest point, the Gokstad ship stands as a tribute to the skill of her builders.

The Viking warship was clinker-built with the hull planks overlapping each other and held together by rivets. The Gokstad ship has 16 strakes on either side and her keel, bows and stern are made of one piece. There are 16 oarports on either side with wooden discs attached to them to prevent seepage of water. There are no thwarts and it is likely that the oarsmen sat on removable benches or on their sea-chests. A mast situated slightly forward of amidships stood directly on the keel and carried a large square

fixed rudder to starboard. Note the supports for the sails when lowered and, of course, the protective value of the shields.

sail. A fixed rudder on the starboard side was manipulated by a small tiller. The ends of the vessel curved up and out and in time of battle were festooned with elaborately carved dragons' heads. A replica of the Gokstad ship was built for the Chicago World Fair of 1893 and crossed the Atlantic in 28 days, going as fast as 11 knots under sail.

The actual longships were of similar design, though we find a raised platform in the forepeak – the beginnings of the forecastle. Longships were classified according to the number of rooms they possessed. A room was the space between deck beams, with each room carrying a pair of oars. Thus the great longships of 30 or 40 rooms

carried 60 and 80 oarsmen respectively. The Viking warship, unlike her counterparts in the south, was not fitted with a ram and battles were decided by hand-to-hand combat; the arms of the oarsman the same as the soldier – sword, axe, spear, and bow.

The most famous of the longships was the 34-roomed *Ormen Lange* ('Long Serpent') built for Olav Tryggvason in the year 1000. It was not the vessel, however, that counted in combat but the manpower and, in the renowned Battle of Svolde (1000 A.D.), Tryggvason was defeated by the overwhelmingly superior force of Sven Forkbeard who subsequently took possession of Norway.

THE STURDY MEDIEVAL COG

Well into the middle ages the ships of northern Europe were modelled on the Viking longship. Then in the 12th and 13th Centuries significant improvements were made, improvements which transformed the oared longship into the sailing man-of-war.

The first of these innovations was the invention of the stern rudder. Hitherto the rudder had been attached to the starboard side of the vessel. This proved admirable as long as the ship was oared or sailed *leeward* (against the wind). But as soon as merchants, for reasons of economy, wished to take full advantage of wind it became necessary to find an alternate position for the rudder. For if the vessel sailed *windward* (with the wind), with the wind blowing starboard, the side rudder would be swept out of the water. Thus the curved stem gave way to the straight stern post to which a rudder could be hung quite easily.

In the south the low-lying galleys operated a double rudder system, one on either side, but eventually the superiority of the stern rudder (in terms of ease of handling and greater control and manoeuvrability) proved itself and was adapted for their use as well.

The second innovation was the deep-draught hull. The Viking ships had been shallow built for greater speed but it was soon discovered, again by merchants with an eye to cargo space, that a ship with a deep hull, though slower, made a much better sailer.

To take advantage of these improvements better sailing techinques and rigging had to be developed. For instance if a ship was *close-hauled*, in other words brought as near as possible to the wind, it was found that the vertical edge of the sail would flap and curl in the wind, reducing its effectiveness. Thus *bowlines* attached midway down the edge of the sail were invented. In smaller ships it was necessary to extend the bowlines beyond the stem, which led to the invention of the *bowsprit*, a shaft protruding from the stem of the vessel.

So by a slow and often laborious hit-and-miss method progress was made. The Viking longship became the early medieval *nef* and that in turn was transformed into the one-masted *cog*. Over two centuries, from the mid 13th to mid 15th, the cog was the most prominent ship, either for war or peace, in northern waters.

An English cog — the stern rudder is now firmly established. Note the grappling iron hanging from the bow-sprit and the castles fore and aft.

The cog, like the longship, was clinker built. On average the keel length was about 100 feet, with a 23-foot beam. The lone mast situated amidships carried a square sail. In later years the *shrouds* (ropes attached to the mast to relieve it of stress) acquired *ratlines* (cross strips of rope), which served as a ladder for the lookout to the crow's nest.

The raised platform of the longship had by now become full-fledged fore- and aft-castles. The castles were turreted fortifications built high at either end of the vessel. They were specially designed for combat use since they enabled archers to clear the enemy's deck prior to boarding. And if boarded by the enemy the castles, mini-forts, were powerful strongholds which could only be taken with the very greatest of difficulty.

The cog proved a sturdy, sea-worthy vessel, an effective compromise between warship and merchant ship. For no medieval king could afford a fleet of specially constructed warships. In times of crisis he called on a levy of private ships which, when outfitted with fore- and aft-castles, were ready for combat.

Crossbows at Sluys

In 1340 the new, improved sailing vessel of the north, in combination with a ferocious weapon developed for land warfare – the crossbow, showed its deadly effectiveness at the Battle of Sluys.

In 1337 hostilities had finally broken out between the French king, Philip VI, and his English cousin, Edward III. Both kings conducted lightning attacks on the other's territory. Philip had plundered and burned the coastal towns of Dover, Sandwich, Rye, Portsmouth, and Hastings. In retaliation Edward seized Thun-l'Eveque and marched into Cambrésis. Philip advanced to meet him and the two armies prepared to do battle. That was in October, 1339, but as Philip had been counselled that his stars were unfavourable and as Edward was fighting a defensive action

The crossbowman wound up his bow by hand. He held the end steady by placing his foot in the ring provided for this purpose. The crossbow was a thoroughly lethal weapon and could achieve accurate results.

The medieval cog went into battle off Sluys in 1340. The high fore- and aft-castles were two of the dominating features of the cog. The illustration is a Victorian representation by James Doyle.

their positions were stalemated. Edward retreated, returning to England on February 21, 1340, to raise more money and more troops.

Philip, anxious to prevent Edward's return with reinforcements, assembled a powerful fleet of 200 cogs, galleys, and barges, with which he sailed to Sluys to intercept the English monarch.

Sluys, today, is an inland city several miles from the sea. In the 14th Century it was an important habour and gateway to the rich Flemish trade. The Flemings, under threat of a blockade of English wool, switched allegiance from the French to the English, thus placing Philip in a difficult tactical position at Sluys. It meant he had nowhere to which to retreat.

Edward, hearing of the French design, gathered an equally large force and on June 22, 1340, sailed to meet his adversary. Two days later

he arrived in view of the French fleet.

The French drew up to the harbour mouth and placed their ships in three lines with the largest vessels in the vanguard. To ensure that the front would not break, the French admirals lashed the ships of the van together with chains and cables. Soldiers were armed with swords and pikes and catapults provided with stone missiles were placed in the castles. One of their largest ships, the *Christopher*, a captured English cog, had a crew of Genoese crossbowmen.

Edward also arranged his fleet in three divisions under the commands of Sir Robert Morley, the Earl of Huntingdon, and the Earl of Arundel. In the arming and placement of his vessels Edward used a favourite technique which had given him decisive victories in the Scottish wars. Men-at-arms were stationed in every other

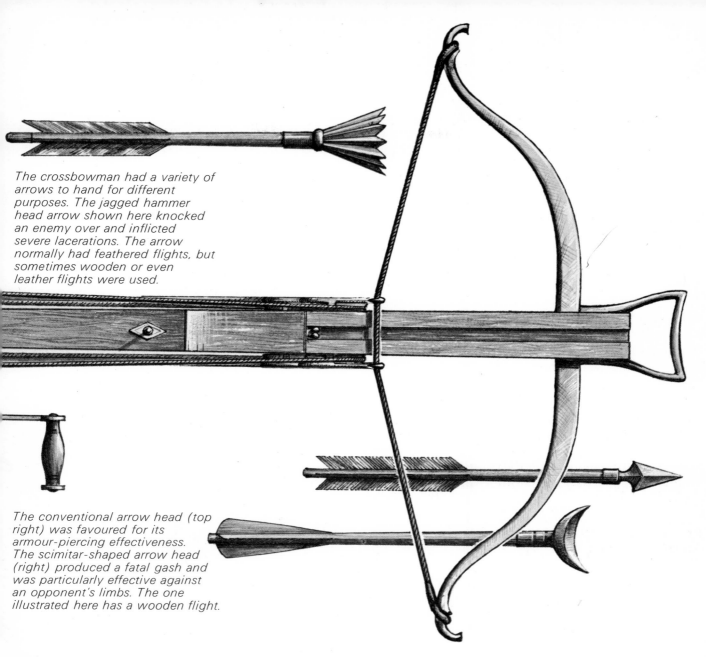

The crossbowman had a variety of arrows to hand for different purposes. The jagged hammer head arrow shown here knocked an enemy over and inflicted severe lacerations. The arrow normally had feathered flights, but sometimes wooden or even leather flights were used.

The conventional arrow head (top right) was favoured for its armour-piercing effectiveness. The scimitar-shaped arrow head (right) produced a fatal gash and was particularly effective against an opponent's limbs. The one illustrated here has a wooden flight.

ship with archers in the ships on either side. The idea was to allow the archers to sweep clear the French decks, after which the men-at-arms, swooping up from the rear, would grapple and board the hapless enemy vessel. The old tactics did not fail Edward in this crucial battle.

The day wore on and Edward made no move. Wisely he waited until all the natural advantages were on his side. Shortly after noon, with the tide and wind in his favour, Edward gave the signal to attack.

Sir Robert Morley was the first to engage, setting the pattern for the battle. At the signal he headed straight for the *Christopher*. The English archers poured an endless and lethal rain of arrows onto the French ship. The archers' work done, the men-at-arms shot up from the rear and grappled and boarded the crippled cog.

In a short while the vessel was taken. The French flag removed, the English raised their own and the *Christopher* was immediately manned and sent back into the fray.

One by one the French ships fell. The French vanguard was broken and soon the rear lines had no heart left for a fight. By sunset the first major battle of the Hundred Years' War was over – a decisive victory for the English. Superior sailing ability in good ships and the fortified castles which enabled the archers to do their work had proved of inestimable value in giving the English their victory. For the next generation, thanks to the cog, England was to control the Channel. Though centuries were to pass before England became mistress of the seas, she had learnt an important lesson about the supreme importance of naval power for her defence.

GUNPOWDER – THE GREAT DIVIDE

In northern Europe the naval powers were experimenting with, and eventually using, sail as the major means of propulsion. In the Mediterranean the classical heritage, the oared fighting ships of Greece and Rome, continued to provide the models for warship construction. Not that there were no developments but those that did occur consistently remained within the sphere of oared warships.

Then, in the mid-14th Century, the invention of gunpowder and the mariner's compass changed forever the nature of naval warfare. In 1260 an English monk, Roger Bacon, had noted a formula for gunpowder – seven parts of saltpetre, five of charcoal, and five of sulphur. It was another 50 years before the first gun appeared, but by 1345 firearms were coming into regular use on the battlefields of Europe.

The introduction of heavy artillery onto warships posed severe technical problems of design. To bear their weight ships had to become much sturdier; to protect themselves from enemy shot they had to become much stronger.

The compass had a similar effect on ship construction. The compass put navigation on a scientific basis. Sailors no longer had to turn their heads anxiously to the sky. The compass gave them their direction and also opened up vast new possibilities of sea exploration. Ships had to be adapted for long journeys and unknown dangers. Again, as with artillery, ship design had to be rethought to meet contemporary needs. In this way, two different approaches merged to produce the next stage in marine development.

The challenge of these two inventions was met in two distinctive ways – the galeass of the Mediterranean and the galleon of northern Europe.

THE GALEASS AND THE GUN

Up to the 16th Century the oared fighting galley retained an honoured place in the Mediterranean world. It had proved its worth in many battles, from the Venetian conquest of Constantinople, in 1204, to engagements in the French revolutionary wars. The invention of gunpowder, however, posed problems which could not be shrugged aside. The time-honoured battle method of ram and grapple had no place in a world where an opponent could keep his distance and still blow the enemy to smithereens. Yet the naval authorities were reluctant to exchange the clean, fast lines of the galley for the bulky sailers of the north. So the galeass was built – a compromise between the oared fighting ships of the Mediterranean and the now dominant sailing ships of the northern seas.

The galeass was to provide the manoeuvrability of the oared ship with the fighting power of the sailing man-of-war. The ship was about 160 to 170 feet in length and 28 feet across, with a draught of 11 feet. It had a displacement of about 700 tons. The galeass was manned by 52 oars, 26 on either side, rowing on the *al scaloccio* system whereby each oar would be manned by

anywhere from four to seven men. It was also rigged with three lateen masts and at times a fourth mast, possibly a bowsprit carrying a small square sail. A protective deck covered the rowers, providing a fighting platform for the soldiers and room for the sailors to handle the rigging.

The most important feature of the galeass was the guns it carried. The galeass was the first stage in the development of the broadside. Of the 30-odd guns on the vessel about 18 were fitted on the sides, spaced out on the deck above the oarsmen. The remainder were placed on the castles in the stem and stern of the vessel.

The guns were a combination of periers (short guns firing stone missiles), cannon (medium length guns firing heavy shot), and culverins (long guns firing medium weight shot). The weight of shot varied between two to 50 pounds. In addition to the heavy guns there could have been as many as 60 smaller pieces on board.

In the end the galeass proved a stop-gap, neither fish nor fowl. It was soon to be superseded completely by sail. Yet it was a decisive factor in the Battle of Lepanto and deserves credit for its fine performance there. The Battle of Lepanto was one of the most significant fought in the western world, for it was there that the threat of a Turkish Mediterranean was crushed forever.

A galeass as used in the Battle of Lepanto. There are gun ports on either side and in the fore turret. There are also smaller guns on the stern rail.

Lepanto — one of history's most definitive battles, in which Don John of Austria defeated the Turks.

Don John – the Victor of Lepanto

On May 25, 1571, a Treaty of Alliance was signed between the Republic of Venice, Spain and the Papacy. Its principal objective was to halt Turkish expansion. The treaty was concluded with a great deal of reluctance and finally only under the pressure of the Turkish advance.

The war against the Turks had the sea as its battlefield and, accordingly, provisions were made to mass a fleet. The 25-year-old Don John of Austria, bastard son of the Emperor, Charles V, and half brother of the Spanish king, was appointed commander-in-chief of the Christian League. The fleet, however, remained divided into its national units and the management of the war would be decided by the vote of the three national generals – Don John for Spain, Sebastino Veniero of Venice and Marc Antonio Colonna, acting for the pope.

In August, 1571, Don John arrived at Messina to oversee the final steps in the mobilization of the allied fleet. Spain supplied 79 galleys and 22 nefs, the pope 12 galleys and Venice 108 galleys, six galleasses, and two large nefs. Nine additional galleys were supplied by Genoa, the Duke of Savoy, and the Knights of Malta. Altogether 208 galleys, six galleasses and 24 nefs gathered at Messina. Though the Venetians supplied a greater number of galleys they were sorely undermanned and poorly equipped. Their major contribution was the six galleasses. In all there were about 29,000 fighting men in addition to the 50,000 volunteers and slaves who manned the oars. In the middle of September the allied fleet put to sea in search of the enemy.

The previous 150 years had seen a tremendous expansion of Turkish power and prestige. Constantinople had fallen in 1453 and the Ottomans had penetrated Europe to the borders of the Holy Roman Empire, holding the Balkans and most of Hungary in their sway. They had constructed a vast fleet which threatened all commerce on the Mediterranean and which in 1570 had conquered most of Cyprus.

At the time of Lepanto the Sultan was determined to make the Mediterranean a Turkish sea. The commander of the Turkish forces was Ali Pasha, a shrewd and vigorous admiral who had shown his fearsome capabilities in numerous campaigns. His second in command was the notorious Uluch Ali. As a young man Uluch, a fisherman native to Calabria, was captured by Turkish corsairs and put to work on the slave galleys. Fierce resolution combined with an innate cunning brought him to the attention of his superiors, while conversion to Islam opened the road to high office. From captaining a galley and then through the bloodshed of many battles he pushed his way to his present position, at 60 years of age, the ruler of Algiers and Tunisia.

As Don John's fleet was making its way eastward news came of the fall of Famagosta, Cyprus' main seaport and the last Christian stronghold on the island. The news incensed the allies and made them even more determined to exact their revenge.

Further intelligence revealed that the Turks had made their way northward to the Gulf of Corinth, anchoring at the entrance by Lepanto. There they halted to replenish dwindling supplies and give their troops rest. At the time of the great battle the Turks had assembled a fleet of about 250 galleys with a crew of about 48,000, plus 25,000 fighting men.

On the night of October 6, the allied fleet entered the Gulf of Patras. It was divided into four squadrons. Don John led the centre in the *Royal* with a force of 64 galleys. To his immediate right and left he kept Colonna and Veniero respectively. The right wing of 54 galleys was commanded by the Genoan Andrea Doria; the left wing of 53 galleys by Augustino Barbarigo, Veniero's lieutenant. The remainder of the fleet formed the rearguard under Santa Cruz, who was later to propose the original Armada plans. The Turkish line was composed of Ali Pasha in the centre, Uluch Ali on the left, and Sirocco on the right.

On both sides fervent prayer and promises of the rewards of success were given to spur the men on to greater effort. To his Christian slaves Ali Pasha offered the promise of freedom if the day was his.

As the opposing fleets faced each other four of the six Venetian galleasses were towed a half mile in front of the main fleet, two to each squadron. The greatest sea battle that the world had yet witnessed was joined on the morning of October 7, 1571.

Barbarigo, on the Christian left, opened the attack. The galleasses, towering over the galleys of both fleets, opened fire, pouring forth a heavy barrage which cut the enemy's vessels disastrously. The Turks had not expected anything like this. Even so they drove into Barbarigo's

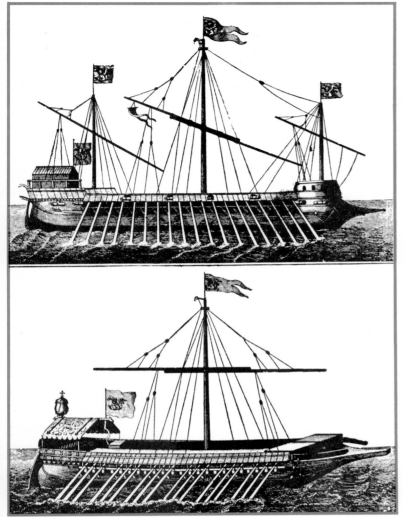

*Above: Don John of Austria, hero of Lepanto.
Left: The type of Venetian galeass used in the
battle of Lepanto (1571). The cannons firing their
deadly broadsides helped to blast the Turks out of
the Mediterranean and opened a new chapter
in the history of naval warfare.*

squadron, avoiding the galeasses and attempting
to outflank the Christians. The tactic worked
and for a while Barbarigo was hard pressed. In
the heat of the battle he received a mortal wound
in the eye but the Christians were rallied by
his lieutenant. The Turks were driven back on
themselves and towards the shore. The Christian
slaves seized this crucial moment to rise against
their alien masters. The battle on the left flank
was a complete rout. Sirrocco was captured and
executed and all his vessels taken captive.

In the centre a similar scene prevailed and
after an hour and a half of bloody fighting the
Turks were overcome and Ali Pasha himself
killed. The lowering of the Turkish standard
signalled the defeat of the Muslems, though even
then they did not immediately give up but
continued a desperate and hopeless battle.

To the right the situation was more complicated.
The galeasses had not had time to form in position
in front of Doria's squadron. He was faced by a
superior force which threatened to envelop him.
Doria was not a popular leader and his inaction
led to the suspicion that he was in collusion with
the enemy. Fifteen of his force, eager to prove
themselves loyal, removed to the centre to take
part in the thick of the fight. Uluch immediately
saw his advantage and attacked the 15 strays,
soon overwhelming them. Doria, furious at being
duped, rushed to attack Uluch in the rear. Uluch
avoided combat with Doria, moving to attack
the Christian centre's right wing with some
success. However, Uluch's successes were too
late and too little to reverse the course of events.
He was forced to flee and made safe his getaway.

The most ferocious sea battle of the world had
been fought and won by the Christian League.
The galeasses had proved indispensable in
breaking up the initial Turkish onslaught,
contributing greatly to the final outcome.

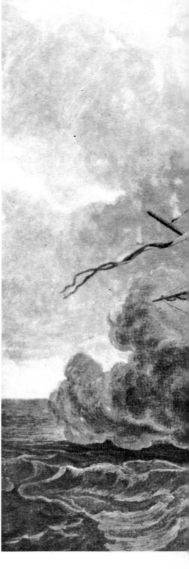

ARTILLERY ADAPTS TO THE SEA

Lepanto was the last major battle of the oared fighting ship. It was a battle fought at close range with ship grappling ship, Spaniard fighting Turk, in close hand-to-hand combat. Seventeen years later the defeat of the Spanish Armada taught the navies of the world that a new method of fighting had superseded all previous ones. The Spanish Armada never came within heavy shot range, much less grappling distance, of the newly developed English galleon. The age of sail in naval warfare had arrived, its inception spurred on by the improved ordnance available for wartime use.

Guns were early introduced into warships but they did not have a central role to play until the beginning of the 16th Century. Until then cannon were too unreliable to be depended on as the sole

weapons. The method of construction (shrinking iron rings over longitudinal wrought-iron bars placed over a wooden core) was primitive and the early cannons were only too liable to shatter under stress. Matters were made worse by the unreliability of the gunpowder. The dried powder used, called 'serpentine', would if left too long either explode or completely lose its efficacy. Thus it was inadvisable to mix until just prior to use and even then the gunners were never too sure what would happen.

Firearms were therefore used only as auxiliary weapons placed in the fore- and aft-castles, where they would serve much the same purpose as the archers of previous years – clearing enemy decks prior to boarding.

The steady development of the gun-founder's

craft over the late 14th and 15th Centuries was to change all that. The forged guns gave way to brass initially and subsequently iron cast guns – sturdy weapons capable of withstanding very considerable stress.

The guns were placed on wooden beds known as stocks. Mobility was introduced with the invention of trucks – small wheels placed at the head of the stock. By the mid-17th Century the gun carriage became completely mobile, with the extension of the trucks to the rear of the stock. Recoil, however, always posed a problem and was one of the most serious stresses that a warship was subject to.

At about the same time that cast guns were coming into general use 'corned' powder was invented. Corned powder was wet gunpowder rolled into tiny pellets. Not only was it safer to handle than serpentine powder, it also gave a much better performance. This was very necessary if artillery was to assume the main burden of fighting in the future.

The Blast of the Broadside

The promise of artillery was realized by Henry VIII of England. He was the first European monarch to be aware of the great changes about to take place in naval warfare and did much to promote those changes. His policies set the foundation for England's rise to supremacy on the high seas. He seized upon the gun and broadside (gunports cut in the sides of the hull) as of crucial importance for the new warfare, which indeed they were. He imported guns from the best smiths in Europe and strove to establish gun-founding as a flourishing craft in England. He made sure that his warships were fitted with broadside armament.

THE GALLEON – WARSHIP OF AN ERA

The improvements in ordnance, the introduction of broadside fire, and the subsequent changes in ship construction marked the dividing point between the ancient and modern in naval warfare, between naval warfare as an extension of land combat and naval warfare as an entity in its own right. Henceforth navies began to form a separate and very important arm (in the English case, dominant) of a nation's military forces. And the ship that formed the backbone of the modern navy was the galleon.

The galleon, as one naval historian put it, 'changed the naval art from its medieval to its modern state'. Not until the advent of steam was there to be such a major technological upheaval in the warship. Under the direction of Sir John Hawkins the galleon became the leading warship of Elizabethan England. Variations on the galleon spread across Europe to form the proto-types of the classical European warship (the ship-of-the-line) of the 17th and 18th Centuries.

The galleon was a smaller ship than the older carrack. It displaced a mere 500 tons but more than made up for smallness by speed and immense sea-worthiness. The galleon was built long (length three times the beam) and lay low in the water. As shipwrights still avoided cutting gunports through the wales – timber strips used to strengthen the hull – the decks were not flush but broken into short sections with connecting steps. The bottommost deck, known as the *orlop*, was built just below the water-line and was used as storage room. Above it was the main or gun deck. The gun deck carried the heaviest pieces of artillery – on average 16 culverins, seven on either side and two in the stern. The upper deck carried the medium sized cannons (14 demi-culverins and sakers).

The forecastle at the bow and the half-deck and poop deck at the stern were semi-fortified areas, as in earlier vessels. But even here changes had occurred. In the age of grapple and board, the lofty forecastle, though a hindrance to the sailing quality of a vessel, made sound military

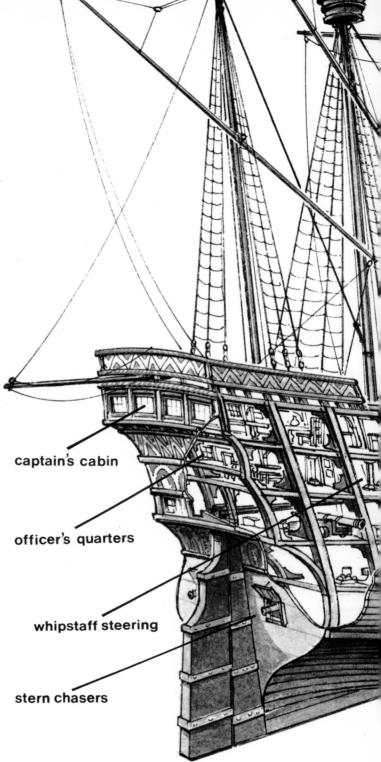

captain's cabin

officer's quarters

whipstaff steering

stern chasers

sense. Not so in the age of artillery and the broadside. So we find the forecastle on the galleon built low and set well back from the stem. The space below the half-deck served as officers' quarters.

The normal complement for the galleon was about 340 sailors, 40 gunners, and 120 soldiers. No quarters were provided for the men and they placed themselves wherever possible on deck.

That the galleon was superior to the Mediter-

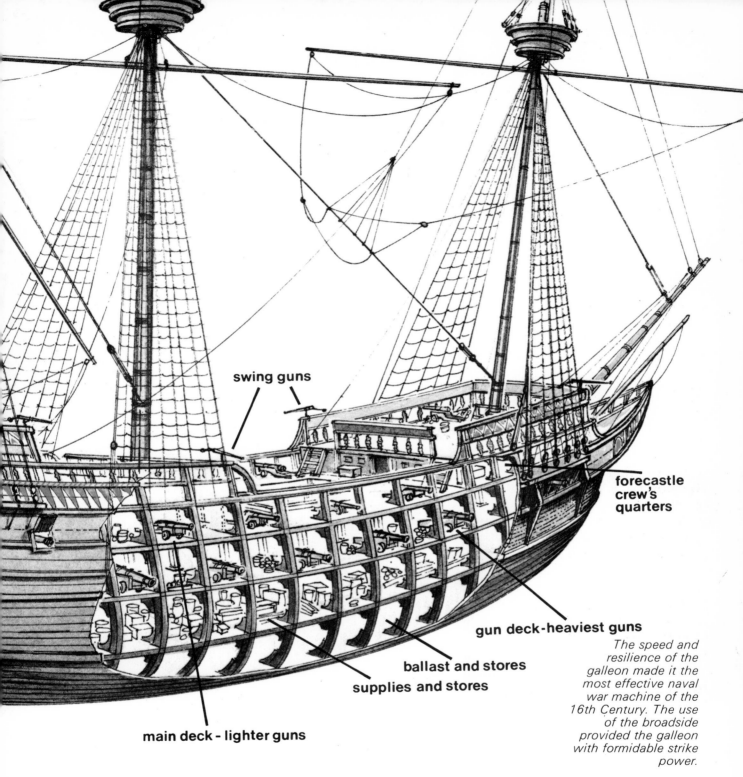

swing guns

forecastle
crew's
quarters

gun deck-heaviest guns

*The speed and
resilience of the
galleon made it the
most effective naval
war machine of the
16th Century. The use
of the broadside
provided the galleon
with formidable strike
power.*

ballast and stores

supplies and stores

main deck - lighter guns

ranean galley was shown by Drake's famous raid
on the port of Cadiz in 1587. With four galleons,
only two of them royal ships, he challenged
12 of Philip II's (the king of Spain) finest royal
galleys to battle. The conditions were perfect for
galley warfare – a calm sea in confined waters.
The Spaniards unhesitatingly rushed the English
marauder. Drake manoeuvred out of range and
then gave the order to fire. The battery of guns
let loose its deadly charge. Two galleys were

sunk, the rest scuttled back to safety. The English
devil had the best of them. The reason: Drake's
formidable broadside fire (35 battery guns on
his flagship) did not allow the galleys to come
within ramming range. It was a decisive and
important victory. The rising star of the galleon
in naval warfare could no longer be denied.
It took the defeat of the Spanish Armada,
however, to set the cap-stone to Drake's convincing argument at Cadiz.

Above: The English launch the fire-ships at the Spanish Armada, nestled in Calais harbour.

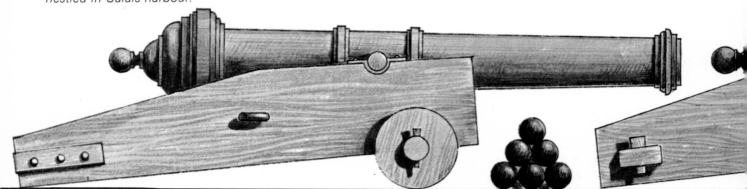

The Spanish Armada

The Spanish Armada was the culmination, but not the termination, of years of hostility. The conflict was a basic one – money. Who was to control the seas and thus the all-important access to the riches of the newly established colonies both in the east and west? Spain and Portugal were the first imperial powers but then Spain annexed Portugal which left Spain as the dean of imperial Europe.

At the same time England, just beginning to flex her naval muscles, was anxious to claim a share of the wealth. So, daring buccaneers, really little more than pirates, of the ilk of Drake, Hawkins and Frobisher, set about plundering Spain's cargo vessels. They, however, aspired to higher things than a mere buccaneering career. They wanted to prove their and England's naval strength in an all out war with the hated rival.

Elizabeth I was somewhat more cautious. Spain, after all, was the most powerful European kingdom, if not the most powerful kingdom in the world. It would not do to tax her too much. Yet, while Elizabeth negotiated, Drake provoked.

In the end there was nothing Philip II could do but go to war. Religion was invoked. The Catholic Philip, zealous for the faith, prepared to conduct a holy crusade against the Protestant jezebel of the north.

Philip was not stupid and he learned the lesson of Cadiz well. The original 1586 Armada proposal was based on a belief in the continued pre-eminence of the galley in combination with those compromise ships – the galeasses. The Armada actually assembled in 1588 was radically different. The galleys were scrapped and in their place stood 73 galleon warships (only 24 were Philip's own, the rest were mainly Portuguese and Castilian), 41 merchant ships adapted for war, four Neapolitan galeasses, and four Portuguese galleys which never reached England.

The English, with 197 ships (which varied greatly in fighting power), matched Spanish strength in ships. The crucial difference lay in armaments. The Spaniards banked their hopes on the short range but heavy-shotted cannon; the English depended on the long range but medium shotted culverin.

Lord Howard of Effingham commanded the English fleet, which lay in wait at Plymouth.

The English routed the Armada with the long range culverin on the left. The Spaniards relied in vain on the heavier shot and shorter range of the cannon on the right.

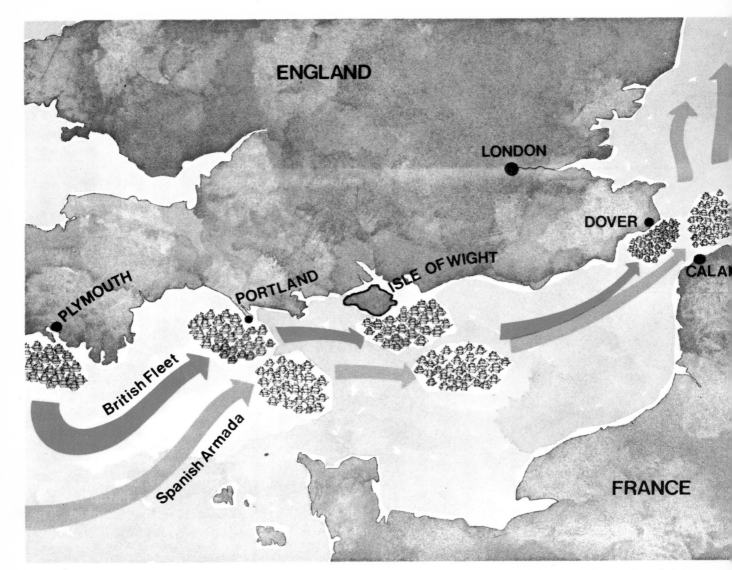

For 11 days the English fleet harassed the Spanish Armada from the rear, as it struggled up the Channel to Calais.

His Vice-Admirals were the fearsome triumvirate, Drake, Frobisher and Hawkins.

The Spaniards rounded the Lizard, off the Cornish coast, on July 19, 1588. The Spanish Commander-in-Chief, the Duke of Medina-Sidonia, held the right centre with the Portuguese men-of-war. On his left, Diego Flores de Valdez led the Castilian force. To the rear and left was the vanguard (an infantry term which had no relevance in the naval battle) under De Leyva. To the left of De Leyva was the rearguard under the command of Recalde. In the centre for protection were placed the hulks and store ships. The overall configuration was of a quarter moon with the horns trailing west.

The first day of contact proved the consummate sailing skill of the English. Tacking hard against the wind they rounded the enemy, unnoticed, gaining the advantageous windward side. With-

out firing a shot the English had won a splendid tactical victory.

English tactics were to harass the enemy from the rear, break their tight formation, and then close in for the kill. For 11 days the Spaniards beat up the channel, dogged by the English who remained well out of range of the heavy Spanish guns. Several skirmishes, one off Portland, another off the Isle of Wight, ended in stalemate.

The English guns could damage but not cripple the Spanish fleet; the Spaniards, on the other hand, could not hurt the English but their formation remained solid.

Unable to establish a base on the Isle of Wight Sidonia decided to make towards Calais to await support from the Duke of Parma. This was his fatal move. The English saw their advantage and took it. Eight fire ships, loaded with gunpowder and other combustible matter, were

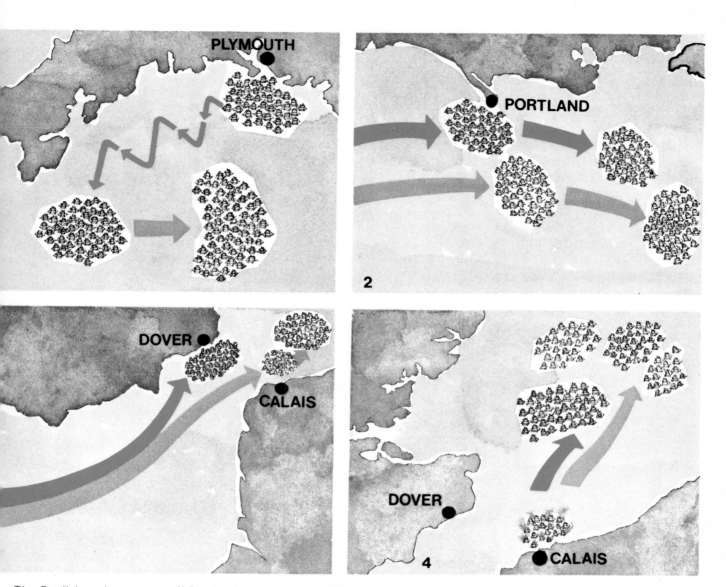

The English make contact off Portland and the Isle of Wight. Fire ships drive the Armada from Calais.

prepared and sent floating into the massed Spanish fleet.

Nothing was more feared in the age of the wooden ship than fire. Not only were the ships very susceptible to destruction by fire but also nothing caused more agony in terms of human suffering. The sight of those horrendous fire ships, possibly set to explode, created an immediate and dangerous panic in the Spanish fleet. There was nothing the Spanish commanders could do to stop the sudden rush to clear the harbour. Cables were cut and anchors jettisoned as ships fought to reach the supposed safety of the open sea.

None of the fire ships reached their targets but the English had achieved their objective. The Spanish formation was broken, leaving them open prey to the English. All hopes of a Spanish victory were dashed. The best Sidonia could

hope for was a safe return home.

That was the beginning of Sidonia's hardest fight. Unable to beat against an adverse wind and a hostile English fleet, he had no choice but to brave the treacherous North Sea. 'The troubles and miseries we have suffered cannot be described to your Majesty,' wrote the unfortunate Duke to Philip. And he was by no means exaggerating. The route home, over the top of Scotland, was a long and arduous one. Many of the ships were wrecked off the Scottish and Irish coasts and the survivors of the wrecks butchered mercilessly by local inhabitants. Of the 130 ships which set sail from Lisbon only 67 returned. The English did not lose a single ship. The Armada proved conclusively that the galleon, properly armed and handled, would dominate the high seas. Henceforth all who aspired to be naval powers equipped their fleets with galleons.

THE DUTCH THREAT

While Philip II was still planning the great Armada his Dutch provinces rose in revolt. The Dutch were a strong-willed and adventurous people who had long depended on trade for their livelihood. Immediately independence was established they were sending ships to the far east. In 1595 four ships set sail for the East Indies, thus setting the foundations for Holland's considerable colonial empire.

A good navy was the necessary corollary and result of trade and colonies. The Dutch were not too proud to learn from their soon-to-be-rivals, the English. It was not long before Holland had assembled a fleet of galleons.

To service the shallow bays and inlets of her country the Dutch galleon was built slightly smaller than the English variety (only two gun decks) and of shallower draught. It made the galleon a better sailer but weaker in war.

In the meantime the English had developed the first full-fledged three-decker galleon – the 100-gun *Sovereign of the Seas*, built for Charles I by the famous shipwright Phineas Pett. The *Sovereign of the Seas*, with a keel of 127 feet, a beam of 48 feet and draught of $23\frac{1}{2}$ feet, was the largest ship ever constructed to that date (1636). In addition to its size, it was also one of the most richly decorated – the work of the master carver, Gerard Christmas. Her ornate gilding led her to be called 'The Golden Devil' by the Dutch, whom

she fought in many battles. An overturned candle sealed her fate and she went up in flames in 1696.

The English were also improving the ordering of their whole fleet. The mid-17th Century saw the introduction of the ratings system. The decision to use in-line-ahead battle formation meant that *ships-of-the-line* (those directly facing the enemy) would have to be of approximately the same strength. The old maxim applied here: clearly, the line would only be as strong as its weakest ship.

A first rate ship had over 90 guns, a second over 80, a third over 50, a fourth over 38, a fifth over 18, and a sixth over six. The first three rates were considered strong enough to fight in line.

Changes were made in the rating system but a classification norm had been established for use over the next three centuries which was invaluable as navies grew increasingly complex and organization became vitally important.

It was almost inevitable that the two small but powerful and very plucky trading nations of the north should come to arms. A Dutch captain wrote after the first Anglo-Dutch War (1652–1654), 'the trade of the world is too small for us two, therefore one must down'. Three times the English and the Dutch fought each other and though in the end the English asserted their superiority it was not always a certainty that they would defeat their dogged enemy.

Left: The splendid vigour of an English three-decker running in full sail before the wind. Note its fearsome broadside capacity. Above: One of England's most famous ships of all time – the Sovereign of the Seas *which combined the design skill of Phineas Pett and the decorative genius of Gerard Christmas.*

THE RISING FRENCH NAVY

Among the many achievements of Cardinal Richelieu, the great French statesman, was the creation of the French navy. In 1624 he ordered a fleet of five warships from the Dutch. Those warships formed the nucleus of the French navy and the models for French shipwrights. By the late 1630s France had built up an Atlantic fleet of 38 war vessels, including the great ship *Couronne*. The 72-gun *Couronne* was France's answer to the English *Sovereign of the Seas* and, though smaller than her English counterpart, could fire as many deadly broadsides.

The French galleon proved to be a better sailer than either her Dutch or English equivalents. She was shallower of draught and wider of beam, making her main gun deck a better platform for the artillery. The 70-gun two-decker became the standard first rate French warship and when properly handled was more effective than any rival vessel. Indeed, the French vessel so impressed the English that they were led to make copies, and captains fought for the privilege of commanding captured French ships.

The Purpose-built Bomb Ketch

The improved galleon was not the only French contribution to naval warfare. In 1682 the pirate town of Algiers on the north coast of Africa was devastated by the French naval hero Abraham Duquesne. The ordinary fire power of a warship could damage but not destroy a protected harbour. To accomplish his aims Duquesne adapted a land weapon for naval use – the mortar. Mortars had been considered too heavy and unwieldly for use on the sea. A mortar-carrying ship would lose all mobility and be at the mercy of hostile vessels. Yet, Duquesne reasoned, in a static situation requiring heavy bombardment nothing could be more ideal than the mortar. The result was the bomb ketch.

The bomb ketch was a broad, sturdy vessel with the foremast removed to make room for two heavy mortars. Heavy beams supported the gun deck and distributed the shock of the recoil. The mortars fired the incredibly heavy 200 pound shot (compared to the average of 60-pounders for heavy cannon). The bomb ketch was heavy and difficult to manoeuvre but she was a purpose-built weapon, not an all-round warship, and she served her purpose admirably. It was a long time before the pirates of Algiers recovered from the shock of 1682.

The bomb ketch, above, cleverly adapted the normally land-based mortar. In this French ketch the fore-mast has been removed.

SHIPS-OF-THE-LINE

The 18th Century was the great era of the sailing warship. The ship-of-the-line, with its classical simplicity and neat elegant lines, claimed the sea as its natural home. Writers and artists, as well as lesser beings, fell sway to her charm. Old sea-dogs spoke lovingly of their 'Mary', referring not to their wives or lovers but the sailing ship which was their home and life. The ship-of-the-line represented a limit in human achievement. It was both the peak and end of centuries of development.

Throughout the century-long struggle between France and England, the greater part of which took place on the high seas, no major technological changes were introduced either in warships or artillery. The great developments were in leadership and tactics. Thus it was generally agreed that the French had the finer ships but time and time again the English asserted their naval supremacy. Nelson's flagship at the Battle of Trafalgar, the *Victory*, was not a newly-built wonder ship but a somewhat old-fashioned vessel, 40-odd years old and the veteran of many sea fights. This did not deter Nelson from achieving his greatest feat-of-arms.

There were certainly progress and improvements. Well into the steam age fine sailers were being built. Yet these remained strictly within the confines of the genre established so many years before in Elizabethan England.

Copper-sheathing for Protection

One seemingly minor but vital improvement was the use of copper sheathing to prevent fouling of a vessel's bottom. This fouling was one of the most persistent and annoying difficulties that a ship's captain had to face. Not only would fouling involve lengthy and frequent dockyard repairs but a ship's life could be cut drastically due to the rotting of her timbers by fungi.

Many methods had been devised to deal with the problem; none of them altogether successful. One early way of dealing with the problem was to attach a layer of felt and tar on the ship's bottom covered by elm boards. Unfortunately, it so increased the drag on a ship that it was

little used. Attempts were made to use lead sheathing but the electrolytic action of the salt water on the sheathing corroded the rivets. Initial experiments with copper sheathing proved eminently successful but copper was expensive and it was some time before it came into general use. It was to copper sheathing that Admiral Rodney attributed his victory in the 'Moonlight' Battle of 1780. Two years later at the scene of his greatest triumph (the Battle of the Saints) he wrote, 'None but an English squadron and copper-bottomed could have forced their way to the West Indies as we have done'.

Above: Oil painting of the Battle of Trafalgar.
Ships from left to right are: Royal Sovereign, Santa Anna, Bellisle, Fouqueux, Temeraire, Redoubtable, Victory, Bucentaure, Neptune, *and* Sta. Trinidad.

Right: Nelson cut through the French to win at Trafalgar.

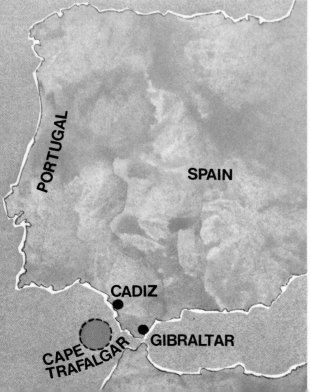

PORTUGAL

SPAIN

CADIZ

CAPE
TRAFALGAR

GIBRALTAR

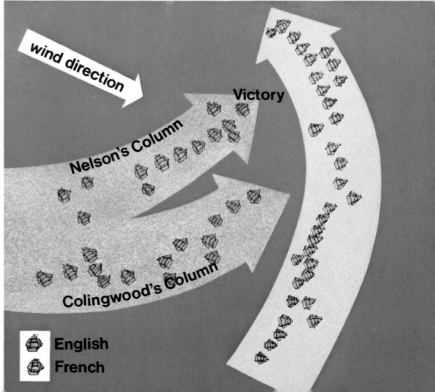

wind direction

Victory

Nelson's Column

Colingwood's Column

English

French

THE CARRONADE 'SMASHER'

The Battle of the Saints in 1782 was important in many respects. Primarily it was a turning point in the history of naval tactics. Nelson called it, 'the greatest victory, if it had been followed up, that our Country ever saw'. Technologically it was important for it introduced the carronade, the first new gun to be developed since the 16th Century.

The ships of the 18th Century had so evolved that existing artillery could do little irreparable damage to them. In battle the rigging was susceptible to damage but the structure of the warship remained inviolable by cannon shot. It was the specific purpose of the carronade to act as a ship-killer.

First manufactured in Scotland in 1778, the carronade was a short, stubby, thin-walled gun with a relatively large calibre. It carried a heavier shot than the cannon but at a reduced range. The carronades were intended to be short range 'smashers', most effective at point blank range, about 400 yards for a 68 pound shot and about 200 yards for a 12 pounder.

The carronade used a smaller amount of powder than the cannon but to greater effect. Unlike the cannon most of the explosive charge was not wasted in *windage* – the space between the shot and the sides of the gun. The small amount of powder used also had the added advantage of ease of recoil. This substantially lessened the stresses upon its mounting and supporting structure.

The first carronades found an eager market in the merchant marine. Especially popular were the smaller carronades of 24, 18, and 12 pounders. But they soon found their way onto the men-of-war and for a time some ships were exclusively fitted with the new weapon.

The great disadvantage of the carronade was, of course, its limited range. Eventually, this consideration led to its being scrapped. Yet in its initial engagements the element of surprise more than made up for the deficiency, as in the Battle of the Saints.

The Battle of the Saints

The French admiral, Comte de Grasse, was jubilant. He had just defeated the British at the crucial battle of Chesapeake Bay. He could now hope to sweep the Caribbean clear of his hated rivals. His next objective was therefore Jamaica, the British stronghold in the West Indies. If Jamaica fell the lesser islands would follow suit. It was imperative to Britain that de Grasse be stopped.

The man chosen to do the job was Admiral George Lord Rodney, capable but capricious and often ailing. With 37 ships-of-the-line he made his way to Gros Islet Bay in St. Lucia where he anchored and awaited news of French movements. He had not long to wait.

De Grasse had stationed himself at Fort Royal, Martinique, conducting lightning raids on the British-owned Leeward Islands. By April, 1782, he had assembled 36 ships-of-the-line and enough troops to conquer Jamaica. On Tuesday, April 8, the French fleet emerged from Fort Royal and headed north to collect more of their trade from Guadeloupe. Rodney was notified of the French move and set off in pursuit. The next day sporadic gunfire was exchanged between the hostile fleets but battle was not engaged. Towards late afternoon a fresh breeze enabled the French to disengage and continue their way northwards.

The winds, however, were uncertain and progress slow. April 12 found the French just south of the Saints islets – their northward path blocked by the islands. A few miles south of the French lay the British, north of Dominica. De Grasse had little choice but to force his way

The Battle of the Saints, 1782. The British close in.

GUADELOUPE

THE SAINTS

DOMINICA

French Fleet

MARTINIQUE

British Fleet

ST. LUCIA

THE SAINT IS.

French Fleet

British Fleet

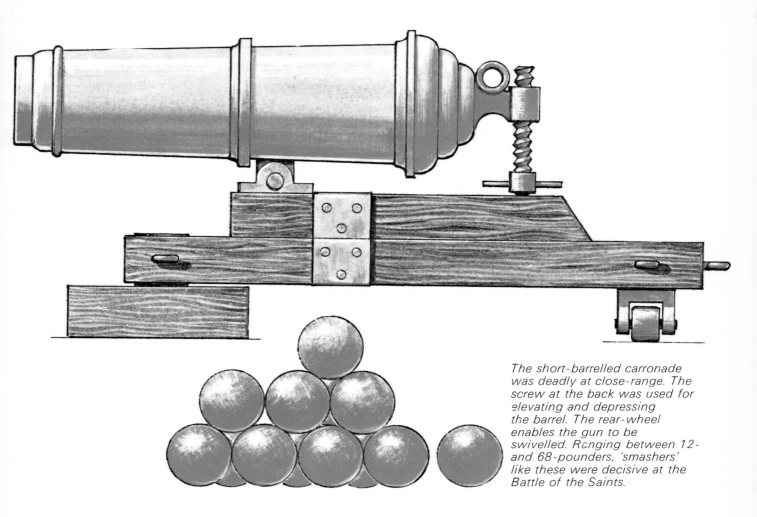

The short-barrelled carronade was deadly at close-range. The screw at the back was used for elevating and depressing the barrel. The rear-wheel enables the gun to be swivelled. Ranging between 12- and 68-pounders, 'smashers' like these were decisive at the Battle of the Saints.

southwards, windward of the British fleet.

Orders were given to form the battle line. The French vanguard of 10 ships was under the command of the intrepid Bougainville; the centre was held by de Grasse and the rear brought up by de Vaudreuil.

Reports of the French manoeuvre soon reached Rodney, who wasted no time in getting his fleet into line. Rear-Admiral Drake led the vanguard, Rodney kept the centre, and Rear-Admiral Hood took the rear.

De Grasse was in a difficult situation. He had not dictated the battle conditions and he would be forced to pass the British at close quarters – ideal for carronade use.

At about 7.30 on the morning of the 12th the van of the two fleets made contact. The French began firing from extreme range. Captain Penny, in the lead of the British van, held fire until he was within 400 yards of the enemy. The signal was then given and the 'smashers' discharged their destructive burden.

Penny bore away to lead along the French line while the rest of his division followed suit. Half an hour later the *Formidable*, Rodney's flagship, was in the thick of the fight. Rodney's main concern at the time was to contract his line even further and to close the range. Carronade fire was most effective at 200 yards or even less.

The French ships received a brutal beating but still had hope of gaining their objective. A shift of wind was to dash those hopes. The 74-gun *Glorieux* was taken aback and forced leeward. A gap opened in the French line. Seizing his opportunity Rodney forced his way through the gap, carronades blazing. Soon a second and a third break was made in the French line. The British had gained the windward side, thus breaking the back of French resistance. With the capture of de Grasse's flagship, the *Ville de Paris*, Rodney called a halt to the bloodshed. So it was that with the help of the carronade Rodney opened a new chapter in naval history.

THE FRIGATE – LIGHT AND FAST

One 18th Century development which we can only mention briefly was of vital importance for the new kind of naval warfare: the introduction into European navies of the frigate and corvette class of warships. Nelson had cried out in 1798, 'Were I to die this moment, want of frigates would be found engraved on my heart!' As tactics, rather than superior technology, became the all important factor in naval warfare there was a greatly increased need for light, fast warships that could be used for convoy and reconnaissance duties.

The early frigates were one-decked warships carrying 24 to 28 guns with a crew of about 160. They gradually grew in size until the largest English ones carried 44 guns. The French-designed frigates were among the finest in the world and served as models for those of other nations.

The frigate was the basis of the early American navy, serving it in good stead in the War of Independence and the War of 1812. In the last decade of the 18th Century three of the world's largest frigates were built in the United States – the *United States* and the *Constitution* (both launched in 1797) and the *President* (launched 1800). These frigates had a keel of 146 feet, a beam of 44 feet and supported 30 long 24-pounders on the gun deck, 20 to 22 12-pounders on the forecastle and half-deck plus another two long 24-pounders on the forecastle.

The corvette (the English sloop) was a class of warship under the frigate serving a similar function. The corvette carried 18 to 20 guns and it was not unusual for them to be propelled by oars as well as sail.

Above: The U.S. frigate Constitution *takes the British frigate* Guerrière *captive in the war of 1812.*

The light, fast frigate was an important tactical machine at the end of the 18th Century, used by all the main warring nations with marked effect.

A NEW FORM OF POWER

The introduction of steam powered engines into ships revolutionized not only construction but the whole nature of naval warfare. Essentially, steam freed a ship to move as it pleased – an obvious advantage for naval commanders. The idea of propelling a ship free from the whims of wind and weather and with greater efficiency than oared power was an old and cherished dream. And for centuries it remained a dream, for the would-be inventors were faced with the seemingly insoluble problem of finding an independent, mechanical source of power. Then came the great scientific and industrial advances of the 18th and 19th Centuries. A means was finally provided to realize the ancient dream; power could be had by harnessing the energy of steam.

The first practical steam engine was patented in 1698 by Thomas Savery. It was a primitive engine utilizing the vacuum created by condensing steam to drive a piston. Though its use was limited to pumping water from mines (the Savery engine was known as the Miner's Friend) it was the first of a series of technological innovations which radically altered the face of human history.

The next step was taken by Thomas Newcomen, a Dartmouth blacksmith. He improved upon Savery's design, creating the atmospheric engine. An overhead beam with arched ends oscillated, by means of a gudgeon, on a fixed support. One end of the beam was connected by a chain to a brass piston which fitted into a large bore, vertical cylinder. Leather flaps were placed round the edge of the piston and water poured on top to form an airtight seal. A heavy pump rod with plunger hung from the other end of the beam.

At rest the piston remained at the top stroke due to the weight of the pump rod. Steam was

Left: Thomas Savery's steam engine of 1696. It was known as the Miner's Friend, because it was used for pumping water out of the mines. This was the first practical use of steam as a source of power, although it was nearly a century before it was used for motive power.

Near Right: A plan of Newcomen's pumping, or 'atmospheric', engine of 1712. This was also used in mines. The downward stroke of the piston, caused by atmospheric pressure on top of it and the creation of a vacuum beneath it, developed the working stroke.

Far Right: It was in working to repair this model of a Newcomen engine that James Watt discovered how to increase the efficiency of the steam engine. It was not long before the new form of power was driving warships across the oceans of the world.

introduced into the cylinder and condensed to create the vacuum. Atmospheric pressure acted on the piston to force it down, thus raising the rod and plunger. When steam was admitted again into the cylinder the weighted pump rod pulled the piston up and the cycle would start anew.

For decades Newcomen engines proved their usefulness in mines across Europe, but the problem of applying steam power to machinery in general was not solved. Watt's double-impulse engine and Pickard's crank and rod were the crucial elements in actualizing the potential of steam power.

In 1764 James Watt, an instrument maker in the employ of Glasgow College, was asked to repair a Newcomen engine. Not only did he repair it, he had soon increased considerably its efficiency by the invention of a separate condensing chamber. From there he was led into further investigations of the properties of the steam engine. The end result was the double impulse engine, patented in 1769.

The first thing Watt had done was to close off Newcomen's open-ended cylinder, replacing atmospheric pressure with steam. Improved though it was it still remained a primitive, single-acting engine. The motive power of steam was not yet recognized.

Watt's next step was the invention of the slide-valve, by means of which steam was distributed and condensed on both sides of the piston at the appropriate stroke. Steam then provided the piston's driving force on both the upward and downward stroke. Gears were fixed to the arched end of the beam and the chain connecting piston to beam was replaced by an iron rod. James Pickard's invention, the crank and connecting rod, converted the reciprocating motion of the steam engine into a rotary motion. The steam engine was ready to try its hand at anything.

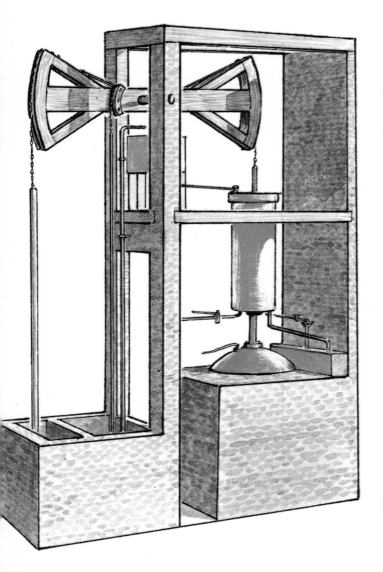

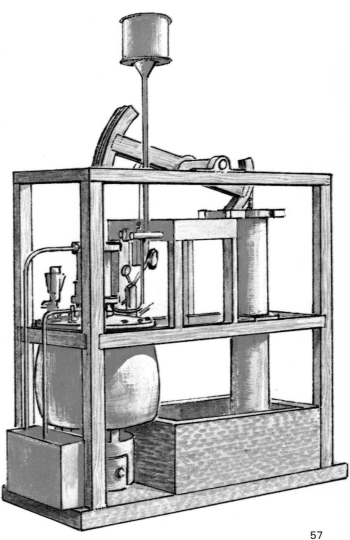

STEAM TAKES TO SEA

As early as 1783 the Marquis de Jouffroy constructed a small steamship, the *Pyroscaphe*, which plied the waters of the River Sâone, near Lyons. The engine turned a paddle wheel set in the stern of the vessel. (Nearly all the early steamships were of the paddle wheel type.)

In 1787 the American John Fitch successfully ran a steam boat on the Delaware River. She was fitted with a horizontal, 12-inch, 3-foot stroke cylinder double-acting engine which drove 12 vertical oars, six on either side of the vessel.

In 1788 a wealthy Scottish banker, Patrick Miller, joined forces with an enterprising engineer, William Symington, to construct Britain's first paddle steamship. The double-hulled boat (one containing the boiler, the other the engine) paddled happily up and down the Firth of Forth at the speed of five miles an hour.

In 1801 Lord Dundas commissioned Symington, Miller's old collaborator, to design an engine for a tug which was to service the Forth and Clyde Canal. The resulting engine was rather unusual for its day: a horizontal direct-acting condensing engine with a 22-inch, 4-foot stroke cylinder.

The *Charlotte Dundas* was launched in 1802, undergoing its first test in March of that year.

Patrick Miller's steamboat, the first paddle boat to be built in Britain. Masts and sails remained.

The diminutive vessel (56 feet in length, 18 feet across) towed two 70-ton boats 19 miles in six hours against strong head winds. The *Charlotte Dundas* was a great technical success but fears that her waves would erode the banks of the canal caused her to be consigned to the dockyards.

The next major developments came from America. In 1807 Robert Fulton built the *Clermont*, a flat-bottomed craft 166 feet in length but only 18 feet in beam. It steamed along the Hudson – the first steamship in active commercial service – at the amazing speed of five knots. The *Comet* (built in 1812) was Europe's first merchant steamship. Rolling along at 6·7 knots she gave regular service on the Glasgow-Greenock run.

The first steam warship was designed by Fulton in 1813. Originally intended to serve in the War of 1812, the *Demologos* was not completed in time to take an active part in the war. She was a double-hulled vessel with a single, stern paddle wheel motivated by a 120-horsepower engine. Her armament consisted of 30 32-pounder guns placed behind 58-inch thick wooden walls. She was also equipped with several submarine guns firing 100-pound projectiles below the waterline. The *Demologos*, renamed the *Fulton*, was never

Henry Bell's Comet *plied the waters of the Clyde for eight years until she ran aground off the West Highlands. Initially, two pairs of paddles were used but it was soon found that performance improved with just one pair.*

tested in action and in 1829 was destroyed by an explosion in the Brooklyn Navy Yard.

Fulton's warship, ingenious though it was, had severe limitations – the limitations of all early steamships – which hindered the acceptance of steam in the navies of the world. Firstly, the large and cumbersome paddle wheel presented too obvious a target for enemy guns. A few rounds of shot could easily disable a steamship, thus removing her main advantage, freedom of movement. Secondly, the heavy machinery of the steam engine displaced the space required for the broadside guns. There would have to be a very good substitute before broadside fire would be sacrificed.

These difficulties, rather than restraining, acted as a spur to further developments. The perfection of screw propulsion and improvements in ordnance heralded the coming changes.

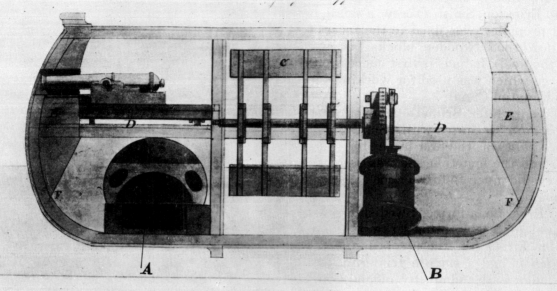

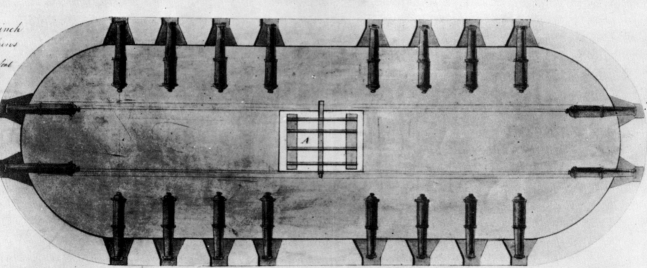

Robert Fulton's design for the Demologos, the first steam warship ever built.
Top: Transverse section. (A) boiler; (B) the steam engine; (C) the water wheel; (D) gun decks;
(E) wooden walls five feet thick diminishing below the water line at (F).
Draught of water is nine feet.
Middle: The Demologos' gun deck, 140 ft long and 42 ft wide, it mounted 20 guns.
(A) is the water wheel.
Bottom: Side view of the warship.

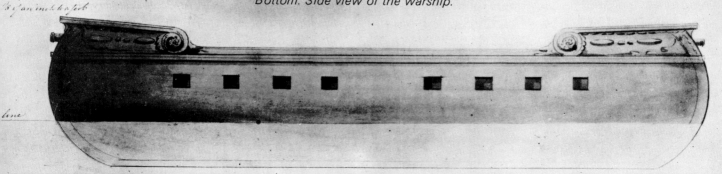

A Tug-of-war for Progress

The changeover from paddle to screw propulsion was the essential innovative factor, making steamships into practical and superior warships.

In 1836 two patents were taken out on screw propellers, one by Francis Pettit Smith, the other by John Ericsson. Smith's screw, a small, helical shaped propeller, was fixed to the recess in the stern *deadwood* (wooden blocks fastened just above the keel). It had its first success on a six-ton barge which was used for working the City and Paddington Canal.

Four years later Brunel's Atlantic liner, the *Great Britain*, was fitted with a Smith screw. The *Great Britain* was the first large ship to be built of iron and the fact that she was supplied with the screw did much to further the cause of screw propulsion.

John Ericsson, a former Swedish army officer, had equal success with his screw, a twin-bladed propeller. Fitted onto the 40-foot launch *Francis B. Ogden* it had a smooth trial run, towing a barge laden with Admiralty officials down the Thames. The officials remained unmoved by her performance but two American witnesses were enthusiastic. They urged Ericsson to emigrate to the United States where his talents, they decided, would not go unrecognized. 'We'll make your name ring on the Delaware,' Captain Stockton told him. Ericsson did not need much convincing and in 1840 he arrived in New York on a small iron steamer fitted with his screw.

Three years later Ericsson equipped the 10-gun sloop, *Princeton,* with a six-bladed screw. An unfortunate accident marred the otherwise smooth running of his invention. An experimental 12-inch wrought-iron gun shattered, killing the Secretary of State and the Secretary of the Navy.

Even with the repeated successes of the screw naval opinion continued to remain divided on the question of paddle versus screw. A practical test was devised in 1845 to see which was the superior of the two. In a series of races the screw-driven *Rattler* proved herself quicker than her paddle-driven rival, the *Alecto*. But, it

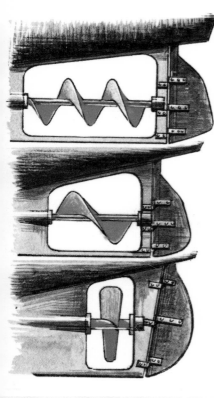

Left: At first it was thought that the longer the screw was the better it would work. At the top, Smith's earliest design of 1836, modified in the centre. At the bottom, Ericsson's improved propeller of 1839.

Below: The famous contest between the paddle (Alecto) and the screw (Rattler) in the North Sea on April 3rd, 1845. Both the 888 ton Rattler and the 800 ton Alecto had 200 horsepower engines. The Rattler, with a Smith screw propeller, proved her superiority by towing the Alecto forward at a rate of 2·8 m.p.h.

was claimed, the paddle had stronger towing powers. That hypothesis, too, was immediately put to the test.

So came about one of the most bizarre tug-of-wars in history. Strong cable lashed the two sloops together stern to stern. The waters churned, the vessels heaved and chugged as the firemen furiously stoked the boilers. Nothing happened. Neither vessel gave way. Then, almost imperceptibly, the *Rattler* inched forward, slowly picking up speed and finally achieving $2\frac{1}{2}$ knots, with the *Alecto* thrashing behind her. The victory was conclusive. There could be no more argument about the superiority of screw propulsion.

One of the principal attractions of the screw for the navy was that the top deck was kept clear for guns and masts. For, until late into the 1860s, steam propulsion was considered simply an auxiliary to sail. 'Down funnel. Up screw,' was a cry familiar to all who served on those curious amalgamations, the steam-sail warship.

HIGH EXPLOSIVE SHELLS

The introduction of the shell gun into the navies of Europe signalled the end of the wooden sailing ship-of-the-line. A wooden ship could not compete with high explosives.

Shells had long been considered too dangerous for use on the ship of the line until, in 1788, Sir Samuel Bentham, working for the Russians, outfitted a fleet of boats with shell-firing brass ordnance mounted on a non-recoil system. At the Battle of Azov the Russian fleet resoundingly defeated a superior force of Turks. The Turkish ships had no defence against the barrage of explosive shells.

In 1822 the French general Paixhans urged the naval authorities to develop the direct-aim shell gun. He prophesied the total eclipse of the sailing ship by armoured battleships propelled by steam and firing explosive shells. The French were hesitant but in 1837 adopted shell guns as auxiliary armament. The British followed suit in 1839 and the Americans in 1841.

RIFLING INCREASES THE RANGE

In 1855 William Armstrong invented a wrought-iron, rifled, breech-loading gun. The Armstrong gun was faster, safer and more accurate than the old smooth-bore muzzle loading rifle. Rifling (cutting grooves into the barrel) gave the lead-coated projectile a spin which greatly increased its range and accuracy. It was not long before the Armstrong process was being applied to heavier guns. However, difficulties with breech-loading retarded progress. Whitworth took up where Armstrong left off and developed a medium weight cannon which, in its trial, proved spectacularly successful. The way was open for the growth of bigger and better guns. As guns grew in size and were more and more protected by armour it became very difficult to maintain the traditional broadside. The advantages of the *central battery* were made quite obvious and it was not long before it was adopted by the great naval powers. At first used in broadside fire the central battery was soon altered to allow for ahead fire. The next major step was the introduction of the armoured turret. The armoured revolving turret gave the big guns full command of the whole sweep of the horizon. John Ericsson in America, Captain Cowper Coles in Britain, and Dupuy de Lôme in France were the men who made the revolving turret a practical proposal.

This massive Armstrong 100-pounder naval gun was of a type that was first tested in 1862. It was made of wrought-iron, had a breechloading mechanism and a rifled bore. Guns such as these introduced a new era of naval warfare. The old, wooden ships could not withstand the power of the high explosive shells.

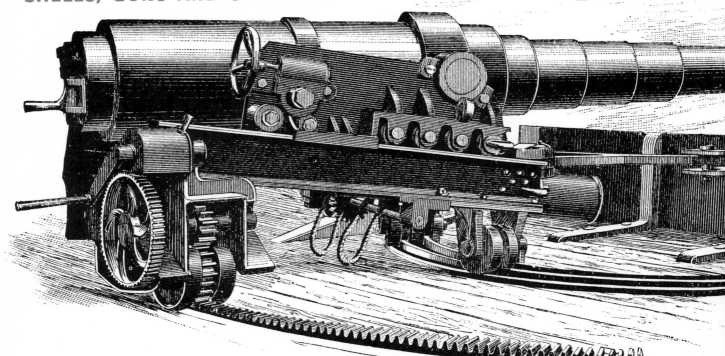

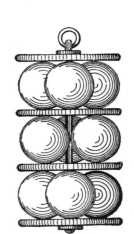

Above: American six-inch steel breech-loading rifle on a swivel mounting.
Right: The French Reffye cannon which was adapted for naval use – see top right.

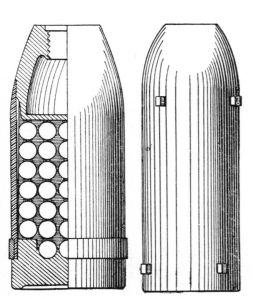

Far left: Shrapnel shell, named after the British general who invented it. The thin shell walls are burst by a fused charge dispersing a quantity of lead or iron balls.
Left: Muzzle-loading studded shell. The studs engaged in the rifling of the barrel thus imparting spin to the projectile.

Left: Grape shot. The iron or lead balls placed on discs around a central rod were covered with a canvas bag. The shock of discharge broke the balls loose but they remained within the bag for a short distance before dispersing.

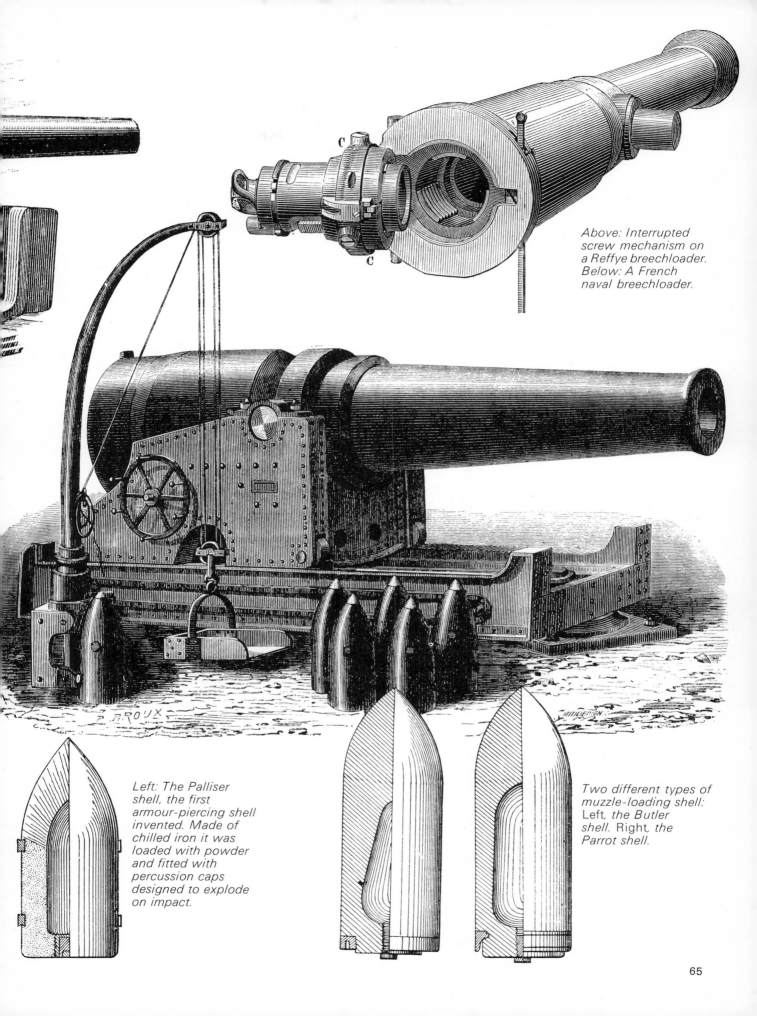

Above: Interrupted screw mechanism on a Reffye breechloader. Below: A French naval breechloader.

Left: The Palliser shell, the first armour-piercing shell invented. Made of chilled iron it was loaded with powder and fitted with percussion caps designed to explode on impact.

Two different types of muzzle-loading shell: Left, the Butler shell. Right, the Parrot shell.

P. B. ROUX

THE MIGHTY IRONCLAD

The ironclad warship was the inevitable corollary to the shell gun. Experiments with iron ships had been going on since the beginning of the century. In 1838 Brunel's transatlantic liner, the *Great Britain*, proved the immense durability of iron. Not only did she operate very well on her run but when she ran aground off Ireland and was recovered a little less than a year later she was found to be barely damaged. The advantages of armour plating in the age of shell fire were obvious. Dramatic proof of its worth was to be had in the Crimean War (1854–1856).

Cross-section of the Great Britain.
1. *Boilers.*
2. *Engines – 4·88 ins cylinders.*
3. *Promenade and state rooms.*
4. *Saloon and state rooms.*
5. *Fore promenade and state rooms.*
6. *Fore saloon and state rooms.*
7. *Officers' berths.*
8. *Seamen's berths.*
9. *Stores.*
10. *Water tanks.*
11. *Cargo.*
12. *Coalroom and berths for the engineers on the upper part of the room.*
13. *Stokehole and fire-place.*
14. *Engine room.*
15. *Shaft of screw.*
16. *Screw.*
17. *Galley.*

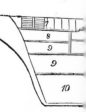

The Great Britain *on her maiden voyage.*

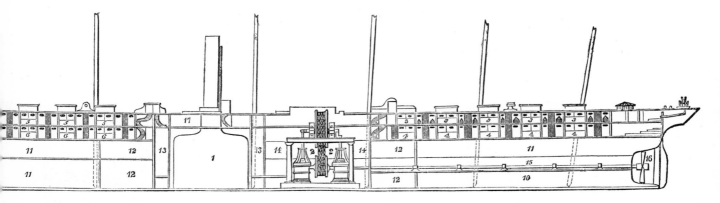

The Crimean War — a Testing Ground

The Crimean War put to the test of war both the theories of shellfire and the ironclad warship. The first test came in a skirmish prior to the war itself. In November, 1853, a Russian squadron replayed the feat of 1788. A Turkish squadron of frigates anchored off Sinope was annihilated by Russian shellfire.

The second test took place two years later. The British and the French had joined forces to defeat the Russian bear. The Kinburn forts were proving an obstinate obstacle in the path of the allied forces. The regular ships-of-the-line could not approach the forts for fear of shellfire.

The French, however, were old masters of bombardment techniques. Three armoured (4½-inch iron plates with a 17-inch thick wooden backing) ships were towed within range of the troublesome forts. The *Dévastation, Tonnante,*

and *Lave* remained impervious to the enemy's heavy firing. The Russian shells exploded harmlessly on their iron sides. The hapless forts, however, had no protection against the French bombardment. Barrage upon barrage slammed into the Russians. In a matter of hours the Kinburn forts lay smouldering, an utter ruin. The French had stated the most convincing argument against wooden walls.

The ironclad developed quite rapidly thereafter. In 1859 the French laid down the ironclad *Gloire*. She still carried three masts and appropriate rigging but by then the sailing equipment was the auxiliary means of propulsion. The British, not to be bested, launched the *Warrior* in December, 1860.

The *Warrior* was the first large iron-hulled ironclad warship. She was fitted amidships with a

The British ship Warrior, *the first large iron-hulled, iron-clad warship. Full rigging was maintained despite the introduction of boilers, smoke stacks and steam engine.*

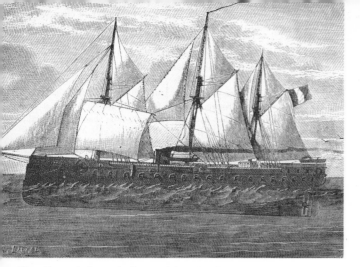

The French ironclad warship, the Gloire.

belt of iron armour 4·5 inches thick. Her armaments consisted of 48 smooth-bore guns, 26 of them behind the armour, placed in the soon-to-be outdated broadside position. Like the *Gloire* she retained full rigging but again only as an auxiliary to her steam engine. She was 380 feet

long and carried a 1,250 horsepower engine giving her a speed of 14 knots. Another unusual feature of the *Warrior* was the iron ram fitted on the bow below the figure-head. The ram was to make a comeback in naval warfare of the late 19th Century. For a while it would prove the only means of sinking enemy ships. The feeling about the renewed importance of the ram received confirmation at the battle of Hampton Roads when the Confederate ship *Merrimac* rammed and scuttled the Union vessel *Cumberland*. That was in 1862. Four years later, at the Battle of Lissa, the Austrian admiral, Tegethoff, rammed and sunk the Italian ship *Re d'Italia*, further impressing naval opinion about the importance of the ram. The ram, however, could not replace the gun. The latter half of the 19th Century saw startling developments in armaments.

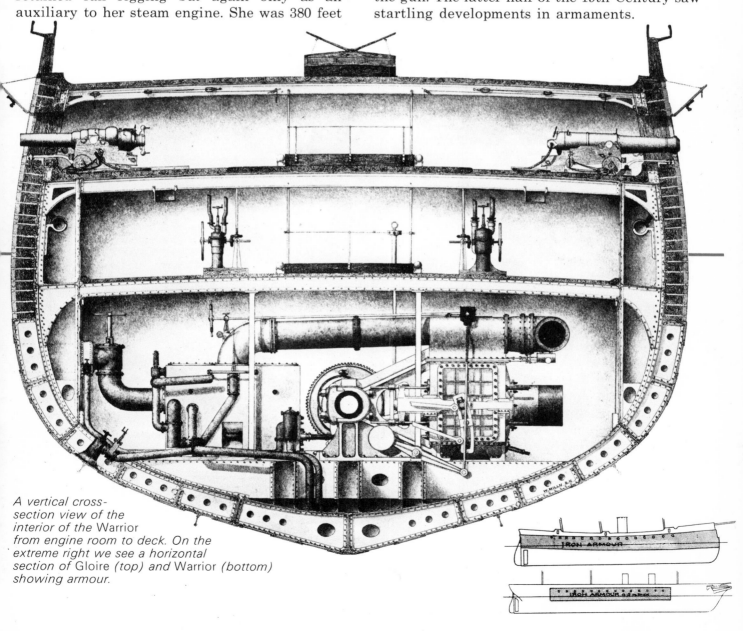

A vertical cross-section view of the interior of the Warrior *from engine room to deck. On the extreme right we see a horizontal section of* Gloire *(top) and* Warrior *(bottom) showing armour.*

THE REVOLVING GUN TURRET

Ericsson, the man who brought the screw to America, in the intervening years had been busily engaged in numerous projects designed to improve warships. A major contribution was his design for the turret ship *Monitor*, built in 1862 under pressure of war. The *Monitor* was powered by a steam engine driving a screw. She lay low in the water and was armoured down to the water-line with five layers of one-inch iron plate. On her deck was mounted a single revolving turret carrying two 11-inch muzzle-loading smooth bore cannon firing solid shot. The turret measured 20 feet in diameter and nine feet in height. The *Monitor* was a strange vessel, hastily built and not very seaworthy. But she incorporated a revolutionary concept which was greatly to influence naval thought in the coming years, especially after the performance of the turret had been tested in battle.

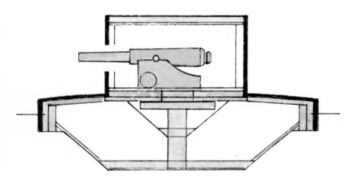

Monitor versus Merrimac

When the American Civil War broke out in 1861 neither side had a particularly strong navy. The Union forces in their retreat from the naval base at Norfolk had scuttled a wooden frigate, the *Merrimac*. The Confederate forces raised the ship and upon seeing that she was not badly damaged decided to convert her into an ironclad. The *Merrimac* thus became the first ironclad American ship as well as the first warship to completely discard rigging. Protected by 16 inches of wood and four inches of iron, the *Merrimac* set out on the hunt. She was armed with three nine-inch smooth-bore guns, a six-inch rifled pivot-gun (all firing explosive shells), and two seven-inch rifled guns placed fore and aft. She was also fitted with a cast-iron ram projecting two feet below the waterline.

The Union forces responded to the challenge by commissioning Ericsson to design the *Monitor*. By March 1862 the *Monitor* was heading south to

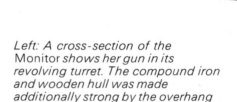

Below: Ericsson's Monitor, *designed and built for the Union forces, was the strangest looking war machine ever to enter battle. But her revolving turret and armoured construction made her more than a mere curiosity. She would have caused immense havoc had she not become locked in a stalemate struggle with her equally well-armoured rival, the* Merrimac.

Left: A cross-section of the Monitor *shows her gun in its revolving turret. The compound iron and wooden hull was made additionally strong by the overhang construction.*

Right: The Confederates raised the sunken Merrimac *and converted her to use against her original masters. She became the first ironclad American vessel, dispensing altogether with vulnerable sails and rigging, too easily ripped and cut by broadside fire. More heavily armed than the* Monitor, *she was as impregnable as her adversary. Union and Confederate navies clashed in the first ironclad sea battle in history and neither side could claim a victory.*

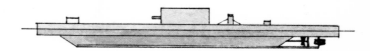

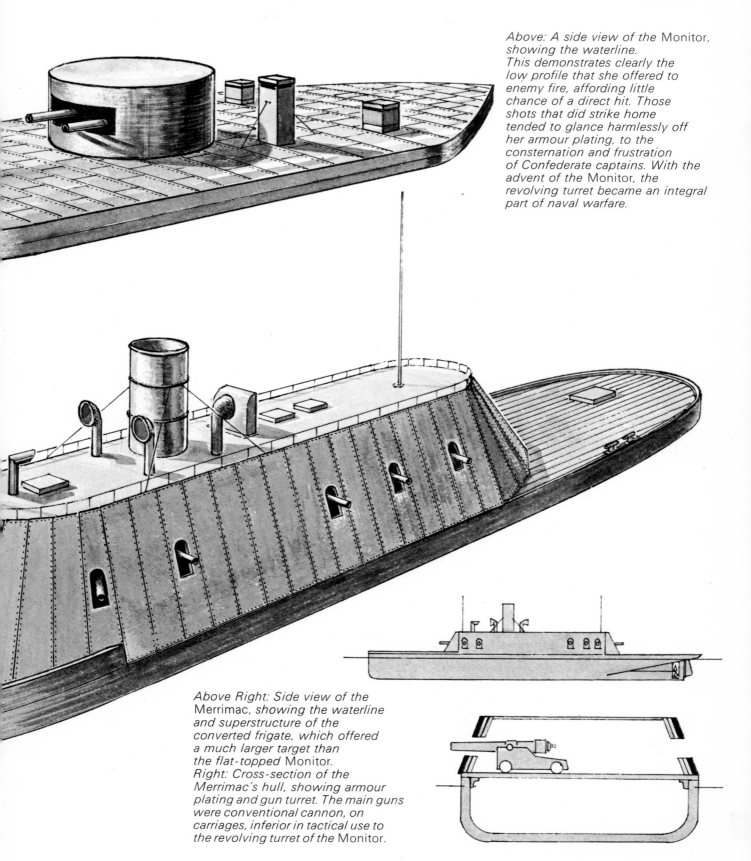

Above: A side view of the Monitor, *showing the waterline.*
This demonstrates clearly the low profile that she offered to enemy fire, affording little chance of a direct hit. Those shots that did strike home tended to glance harmlessly off her armour plating, to the consternation and frustration of Confederate captains. With the advent of the Monitor, the revolving turret became an integral part of naval warfare.

Above Right: Side view of the Merrimac, *showing the waterline and superstructure of the converted frigate, which offered a much larger target than the flat-topped* Monitor.
Right: Cross-section of the Merrimac's *hull, showing armour plating and gun turret. The main guns were conventional cannon, on carriages, inferior in tactical use to the revolving turret of the* Monitor.

challenge her redoubtable adversary.

The *Merrimac*, meanwhile, had just gone out on its first sortie. Steaming out of the Elizabeth River she attacked the Federal warships on the north shore of Hampton Roads. Within a matter of moments the *Merrimac* had destroyed the helpless wooden ships. Their fire bounced harmlessly off her thick armour while she leisurely picked off the *Congress* and then rammed the *Cumberland*. As night fell the *Merrimac* returned to her mooring in Norfolk.

The next day, March 9, 1862, the *Merrimac* returned to Hampton Roads to finish off the remaining Federal ships only to find herself faced with the ungainly *Monitor*. Immediately the two ships began to pound away at each other. The two-gun *Monitor* gave as much as she got but neither side could make any headway. Shells burst harmlessly off the iron sides of the vessels while shot bounced into the waters. By midafternoon the fight died down. The captains of both ships realized they could do nothing against the other and retreated to their respective stations. The great ironclad epic ended in a stalemate.

Although the battle ended in a draw it had important consequences in the naval world. The vulnerability of the wooden ship was once again decisively proved by the *Merrimac's* first day of operation. Secondly, the revolving turret showed itself to be equal to the most devastating broadside fire.

Above: One of the six Dahlgren 9 ins smooth bore guns on the Merrimac. *The gun recoiled on the wooden carriage and was braked by the ropes. The screw mechanism altered the elevation angle of the gun.*
Right: The Merrimac *rams the helpless, wooden sloop, the* Cumberland.

THE BIRTH OF THE BATTLESHIP

The construction of the *Devastation* in 1872 marked the transformation of warships from sailing ironclads into the forerunners of the modern battleship. Prior to 1872 controversy raged between the proponents of the revolving turret and the diehard conservatives who remained faithful to the standard of broadside armament. There were many practical factors which made the turret system appear superior. The use of the naval ram and the increasing size of naval guns were two strong arguments for the switch away from the broadside conception. If the naval ram was to be used in sea warfare then it was essential that a ship fitted with such a device should fire ahead. Likewise, with naval guns becoming increasingly larger to penetrate thicker armour, ships would have to carry fewer guns but these, therefore, had to be able to fire in a great variety of directions.

Sir Hugh Childers, Britain's First Sea Lord, took the plunge and asked Edward Reed to

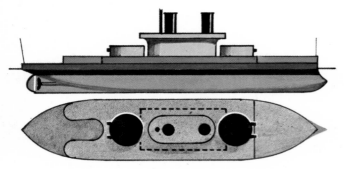

Above: The siting of the Devastation's *gun turrets and, right,* Devastation *under steam.*

design 'a smaller ocean-going turret ship, with a light sailing rig'. Since a contemporary battleship was estimated to require at least 12 inches of armour to halt the penetration of shells, a sailing rig would certainly prove to be a poor second to steam propulsion. For this reason, together with the fact that a sailing rig would hamper the firing of multi-directional armament, the *Devastation* was built solely to be driven by steam.

The design of the *Devastation* was epoch-making. She possessed the rudimentary qualities of the modern battleship, she was iron-hulled, armoured, steam-driven, her guns were mounted in turrets, and of course she was not encumbered by masts, sails, or rigging. She was 285 feet long, 62 feet wide and her twin propellers gave her a top speed of 12½ knots. The *Devastation* was armed with four 12-inch muzzle-loading guns

sited in turrets along the centre-line – one fore, one aft. Each of these guns weighed 35 tons, which, of course, enabled them to fire larger shells, though this raised problems of its own. The increase in gun weight in concentration around the turret meant that the ship had to be more durably constructed throughout to support the gun, and to withstand its recoil.

A further advantage the *Devastation* had over her predecessors or contemporaries was the large volume of bunkering space. Room was made on board for the storage of 1,800 tons of coal. The economical use of her fuel was heightened when a few years later she was refitted with triple expansion engines with cylindrical boilers. In earlier steam-propelled ships the expansion of the steam was done in one or two stages. It was discovered that the economy of the engine would be increased greatly if this operation was done in three stages – hence the triple expansion engine. This engine and boiler enabled steam to be produced at 60 pounds

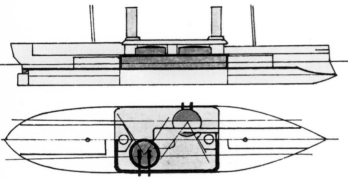

Side view and top plan of HMS Inflexible

pressure instead of the hitherto normal 25 to 30 lbs. For the first time a vessel could cross the Atlantic and return without coaling.

A sister ship to the *Devastation* was launched a little while later. She proved to be even more successful as she was fitted with faster engines and larger guns. The *Thunderer* was also fitted with a hydraulic loading system for her 12·5-inch guns. The guns were depressed until they were over the loading tubes. Hydraulic pressure then forced the rammer, cartridge, and projectile up the loading tube and into the gun via the muzzle. Another novel feature of the *Thunderer* was that these guns could be fired electrically from the bridge.

Although designed as ocean-going battleships, these ships did not take part in any major naval activity apart from minor roles in the Russo-Turkish war of the late 1870s. The *Devastation* was mainly used as a port guard ship, first at

Plymouth and later at Gibraltar, before being broken up in 1908.

Britain's policy at this time was not to take the initiative in naval issues but to counteract the advances made by the other powers. Relying on her efficient ship building and engineering industries, rapid counter measures were employed to produce ships of comparable or greater efficiency. The race for larger armament and thicker armour accelerated at a tremendous rate in the late 19th century. Larger guns were built to penetrate thicker armour, and thicker armour used to combat larger guns and considerably more efficient shells.

The *Inflexible* was built in response to the 15-inch guns of the Italian vessels *Duilio* and

Dandolo. Commissioned in 1876, she was equipped with four 16-inch muzzle-loading guns, mounted centrally in turrets. She had the greatest thickness of armour ever in the history of the battleship. The armour (known as 'compound') was specially constructed for her use and consisted of 24 inches of iron plus 17 inches of teak backing at the waterline, with 20-inch armour plating and 21 inches of teak on the citadel. The *Inflexible* was also one of the first ships to employ an armoured deck. She was fitted with two 60-foot torpedo boats and was equipped with the first underwater torpedo tubes. She was the first ship to be fitted with electric lights, which were run off an 800 volt generator. Her guns were at first worked by pile-type batteries.

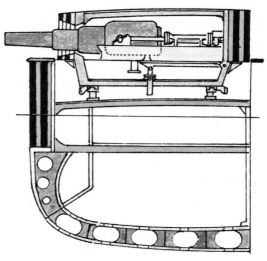

A cross-section of the Inflexible *showing a gun turret and the great thickness of her armour plating. The guns were muzzle loading and could swivel to cover in combination a wide field of fire. It was no longer necessary for the vessel to turn to deliver a broadside.*

Below: The ironclad might of HMS Inflexible.

TORPEDO AND MINE

The torpedo and mine, close relatives, had far reaching effects upon naval design and involved radical changes of strategy during warfare at sea. As early as 1776 an attempt was made to mine Lord Howes flagship, *Eagle*, while anchored in New York Harbour. A man was reputed to have approached the ship in some kind of submersible boat. His attempt failed, however, because the *Eagle's* hull was copper plated.

The first mines to be anchored in sea lanes were made by the Russians during the war of 1854–56. Zinc canisters were filled with gunpowder and set to explode by means of a detonator. The detonator was a glass tube filled with acid which, when broken, would ignite the charge of gunpowder. Luckily for shipping at the time, these mines were too small to cause any real damage.

The torpedo, unlike the mine, does not remain stationary but travels below the surface of the water towards its target, the submerged portion of a ship's hull. One of the more prominent early methods of delivery was that used by the Union officer, Lieutenant Cushing, against the Confederate ironclad, *Albermarle*, in 1864. Known as a 'spar torpedo' it consisted of an explosive charge placed at the seaward extremity of a pole projecting from the ship's bow. The ship would steam towards the adversary and the charge would explode upon impact. Perhaps Lieutenant Cushing should have used a longer pole, because in his case the charge exploded to the disadvantage of both ships.

The British 'Harvey' torpedo also had its drawbacks. The device, towed by means of a long cable was constructed so as to diverge from the course of the towing vessel. But there was no way of ensuring that the towing cable would not foul small boats in the vicinity of the target ship.

The breakthrough in torpedo development came in 1866 with the Whitehead-Luppis torpedo. Invented by Captain Luppis of the Austrian Navy and Robert Whitehead, a Scottish engineer, the torpedo was a long cylindrical case, streamlined for easy movement, with a fairly large explosive charge in the 'nose' driven by a compressed air engine situated at the 'tail'. The early torpedo travelled at a speed of eight knots, which meant that it was only effective at a stationary target at a very short range.

The Whitehead-Luppis torpedo was first used in combat by the British frigate *Shah* in 1877. The *Shah* attacked a Peruvian monitor *Huascar*

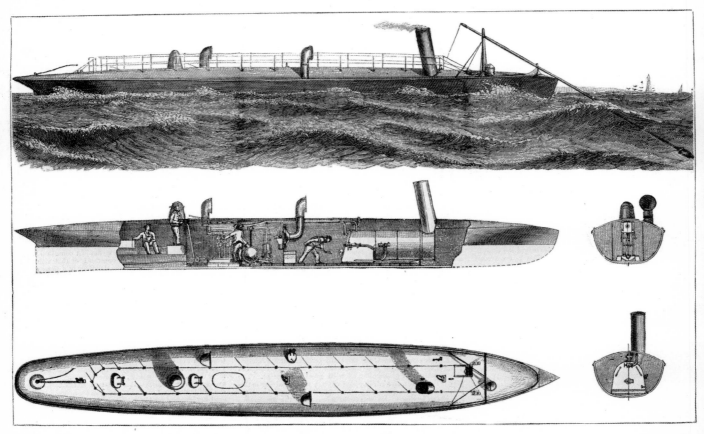

A Russian torpedo boat of 1878. The boat is 75 ft in length and 10 ft across with a draught of 5 ft and a maximum speed of 22 mph. Built on a multicellular design to increase strength and preserve buoyancy in case of enemy fire damaging it, the vessel was armed with three torpedo poles of hollow steel. The torpedoes were either copper or steel cases loaded with between 40 and 50 lbs of dynamite exploded by an electrical charge.
Above: The first true submersible used by the Confederacy, the H. L. Hunley (named after its inventor) was deployed against the Federal sloop Housatonic. It used a spar torpedo to sink the ship but, unfortunately, was itself destroyed in the devastating explosion that followed the impact.

within a range of about 600 yards. The *Huascar* luckily managed to change direction after the launching of the torpedo and escaped.

In succeeding years, Whitehead made changes to the prototype. He further streamlined it and fitted fins which stabilized the movement of the torpedo. He also replaced the gunpowder charge with guncotton which increased the explosive power by three times. Brotherhood's three cylinder air engine was adapted to his later models which gave them a speed of 18 knots. The first successful torpedo attack was launched in 1878 when a Russian ship sank a Turkish vessel in Batum Harbour at a range of 80 yards.

A torpedo attack in the early stages of its history was, to say the least, hazardous. The attacking ship had to steam well within gunnery range to launch its torpedoes. Surprise was of paramount importance during a torpedo attack and a ship making such a move must be fast, elusive and, if possible, invisible.

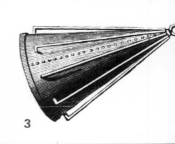

A ship encompassing these qualities was launched by the Admiralty in 1877 – the first torpedo boat. The *Lightning* was 90 feet long and capable of a speed of 19 knots. She carried one Whitehead torpedo which was mounted on davits at the stern. Later the delivery method was changed for a rotating launching tube and shortly afterwards changed again to permanent tubes positioned in the bows. The latter positioning of the tubes meant that she would have to steam towards her target right up until the precise moment of firing.

A point that had been overlooked in the designing of the torpedo boat, and others in her class, was that she was only fit for home waters, thus employing an essentially offensive weapon in a defensive role. The answer was to build larger boats. The slim narrow lines of the first torpedo boats were kept, but the length was increased to 123 feet. The lengthened boats were classed as ocean-going vessels, but not so by the crews who spent uncomfortable days and sleepless nights on manoeuvres with the fleet.

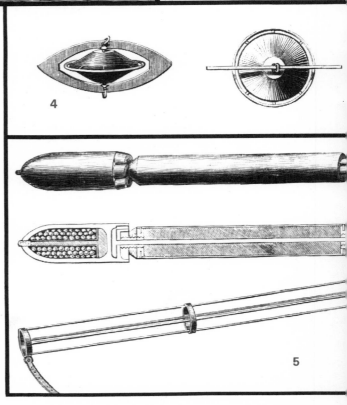

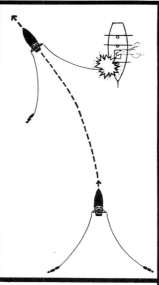

1. *Self-acting electric torpedo. When a vessel hit the guard it touched the plate thus completing a circuit and exploding the mine. (A) the torpedo guard; (B) insulated plate; (C) fuse; (D) battery on shore; (E) wire to earth; (F) wire to torpedo.*

2. *A mine-laying launch.*

3. *Turkish self-acting torpedo.*

4. *Punshon's floating torpedo; left: side view; right: top view.*

5. *Top: Hall Macdonald anti-torpedo-boat rockets. Middle: A cross-section view. Bottom: Rocket carrier.*

6. *Deck of a vessel towing torpedoes towards enemy. The windlasses lower the torpedoes. (Ignore reference letters on this contemporary print.)*

6a. *The torpedo boat approaches the enemy vessel from the south. One such has already veered away allowing towed torpedo to strike target.*

7. *One of the earliest mines. First experimented with in the mid-19th Century and used sparingly in 1917, it came into its own during the Second War. The magnetic field of a steel ship triggers it off.*

8. *An outrigged torpedo-pinnace attacking an ironclad.*

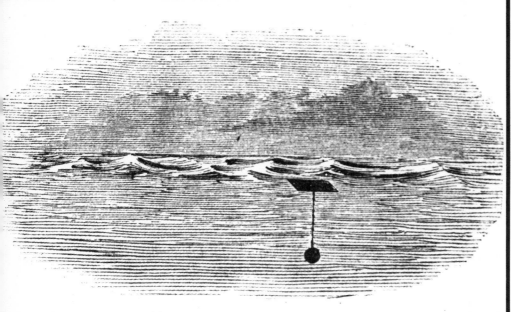

7

8

Top: HMS Lightning, *the first British purpose-built torpedo boat. She was 84 ft 6 ins long, 10 ft 10 ins wide and had a maximum power of 478 hp. She carried one 14 ins torpedo tube and was armed with two Whitehead torpedoes. Middle: The* Destroyer, *a torpedo boat built by John Ericsson for the U.S. Navy.*
Bottom: One of the new, larger torpedo boats built by Yarrow in 1887 for use in an offensive capacity.

Right: A Falke torpedo boat under full power. A torpedo has just been released — note the raised torpedo lid. The Falke torpedo boat carried auxiliary armament fore, centre and aft. Inset, a cross-section showing the general internal arrangement. Note how the bow juts out below the waterline.

TORPEDO BOAT DESTROYERS

The torpedo boat was looked upon by the British navy as a serious threat to blockading squadrons. Many other countries were speedily developing these boats, especially the French, who were constructing extremely fast and very effective models. To counteract the threat of this, Yarrows shipyard obtained a contract to design and build ships that would surpass the torpedo boat. These later became known as 'torpedo boat destroyers'. The torpedo boat destroyers (later 'destroyers')

were designed to be much larger and faster than the French torpedo boats. H.M.S. *Havock*, which was launched in 1893, was 180 feet long and could approach speeds of 26·7 knots. Her sister ship, the *Hornet*, was fitted with the Yarrow water-tube boiler (as opposed to the *Havock's* locomotive boiler), which enabled her to reach a top speed of 27·3 knots.

The water-tube boiler was a major contribution to the advance of naval engineering. In the

HMS Havock.

ordinary cylindrical boiler water was heated in the boiler by copper tubing carrying hot air. The water-tube boiler reversed the process by having the water carried in the tubing which passed through the furnace. The steam pressure was inside instead of outside the tube, leaving very little danger of boiler collapse. The amount of metal necessary to resist bursting at high pressures in the water-tube boiler was comparatively light, though the bigger the bore of the tube, the thicker the metal had to be.

Apart from the overall economy of weight, the small amount of water required meant that steam pressure could be increased much more rapidly than with the cylindrical boiler. This was a very important consideration, for naval vessels were apt to make sudden departures, or fast increases of speed (at the sighting of an enemy), which was difficult with the old-type boilers.

Both the *Hornet* and the *Havock* were armed

with three 18-inch torpedo tubes and one 12-pound and three six-pound guns, giving them all-round superiority over the torpedo boat.

These early destroyers were certainly superior to the torpedo boat on paper but not so during sea-faring trials. Much trouble was reported from the engine room. Apart from signs of hull strain, excessive vibration, extreme discomfort on the part of crew members, the ship was also reported as being too wet and a very bad roller in heavy weather. These troubles were only temporary. Changes in the design of the super-structure and increases in weight displacement made life easier.

Later models, particularly the *Viper*, were widely praised for their fine sea-faring qualities and it was soon evident that a magnificent new type of warship had materialized. The *Viper* had the fortune to be the first naval vessel to be fitted with a steam turbine engine. It enabled her to reach a top speed of 34 knots and was at the time (1889) the fastest ship afloat.

The Parsons steam turbine made its debut at the naval revue held in honour of Queen Victoria's Jubilee in 1897. Steam heated by means of a water-pipe boiler was passed through a series of nozzles, expanding and gaining velocity, and was then directed onto a selection of blades on the periphery of a rotor. The velocity of the steam would pass along these blades, turning the rotor, to power the propellers.

By the late 1870s the torpedo was standard equipment in ships of all classes. Indeed, towards the end of the century, there was speculation that the submerged launching of torpedoes would render the battleship obsolete, as by this time torpedoes were carrying 250 pounds of explosive at a speed of 30 knots.

To counteract the effects of the torpedo, great changes had to be made in hull construction. They were more heavily armoured below the water-line, and were further subdivided by way of bulkheads and water-tight compartments.

For total immunity a steel net apron was boomed out around the ship's hull. When not in use it was hoisted aboard and tied to a shelf constructed on the ship's side – a very awkward and frustrating operation. The immunity conferred by the steel apron did not last very long due to further improvements in torpedo design.

Opposite: HMS Hornet, *sister ship to the* Havock. *Her water tube boilers gave her a faster speed.*
Bottom: The Viper *— a new breed of destroyer fitted with the Parsons steam turbine engine (left).*

WARFARE BENEATH THE WAVES – THE SUBMARINE

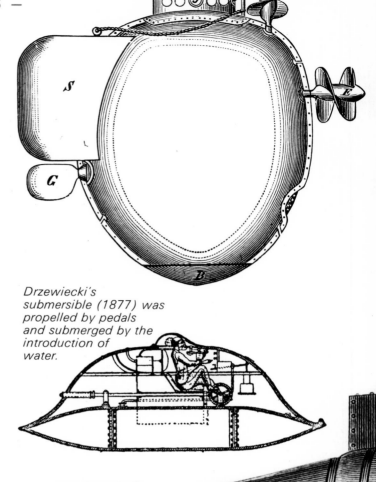

One of the greatest developments in naval warfare was the invention of the submarine. The submarine proved to be the most deadly force in naval warfare since the invention of broadside fire in the 16th Century.

Man has always sought to imitate animals. Birds have long inspired him to fly and fish have fired his imagination with the desire to travel underwater. The idea of building an underwater craft was being explored as early as 1578 when an Englishman demonstrated a submersible boat to King James I. A quarter of a century later, Cornelis Drebbel built a wood and greased leather contraption that could submerge and be pulled about by oars.

The first underwater ship that could properly be called a submarine was built in the late 18th Century. This was a one-man ship designed by an American, David Bushnell, and christened the *Turtle*. During the American War of Independence, it attempted to set a mine under *H.M.S. Eagle*, Admiral Lord Howe's flagship. The *Turtle* approached the vessel, driven by a hand-cranked propeller. The attempt to attach the mine to the copper-sheathed bottom failed, however, and the mine blew up harmlessly.

A hand-driven submarine finally made a successful submerged attack when the *Hunley*, a Confederate submarine, sank the Federal warship *Housatonic* during the American Civil War. Built from an iron boiler, the 30-foot *Hunley* proved a death trap for her crew. In February, 1864, she drove a spar torpedo into the *Housatonic* which was anchored in blockade of Charleston harbour. The subsequent explosion sank both of the ships.

Drzewiecki's submersible (1877) was propelled by pedals and submerged by the introduction of water.

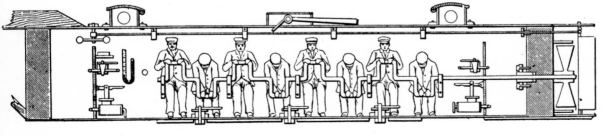

Hunley's David, *one of a number of hand propelled semi-submersibles used by the South during the American Civil War.*

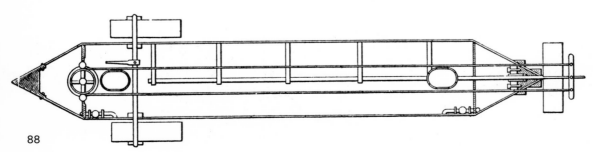

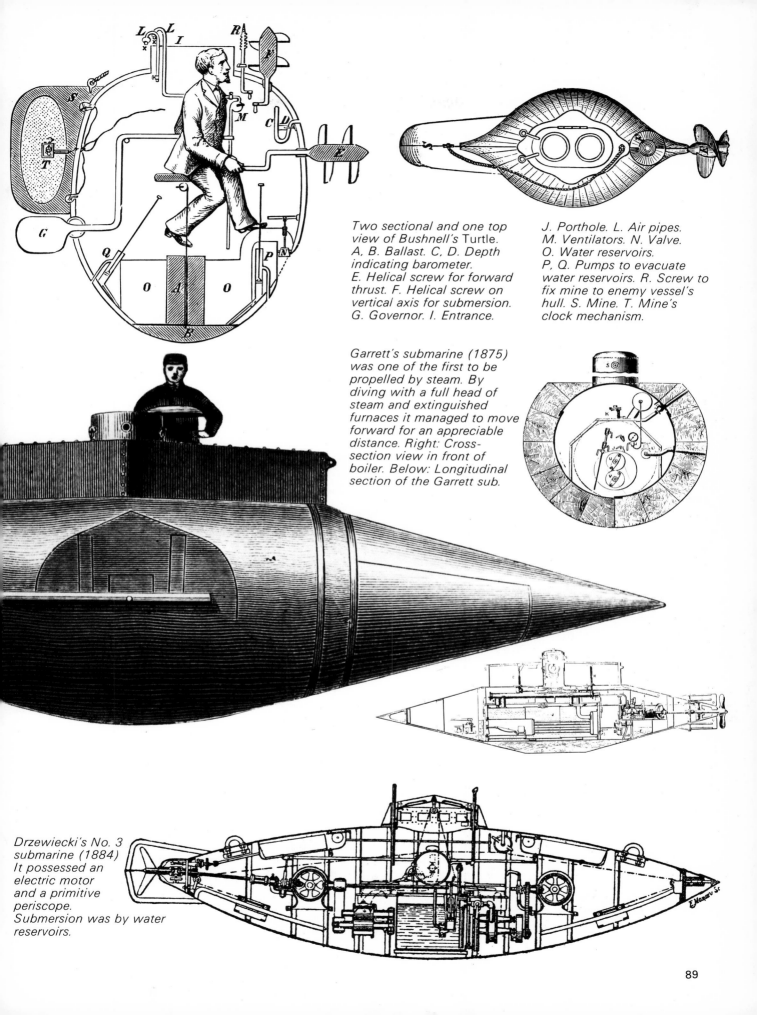

Two sectional and one top view of Bushnell's Turtle. A, B. Ballast. C, D. Depth indicating barometer. E. Helical screw for forward thrust. F. Helical screw on vertical axis for submersion. G. Governor. I. Entrance.

J. Porthole. L. Air pipes. M. Ventilators. N. Valve. O. Water reservoirs. P, Q. Pumps to evacuate water reservoirs. R. Screw to fix mine to enemy vessel's hull. S. Mine. T. Mine's clock mechanism.

Garrett's submarine (1875) was one of the first to be propelled by steam. By diving with a full head of steam and extinguished furnaces it managed to move forward for an appreciable distance. Right: Cross-section view in front of boiler. Below: Longitudinal section of the Garrett sub.

Drzewiecki's No. 3 submarine (1884) It possessed an electric motor and a primitive periscope. Submersion was by water reservoirs.

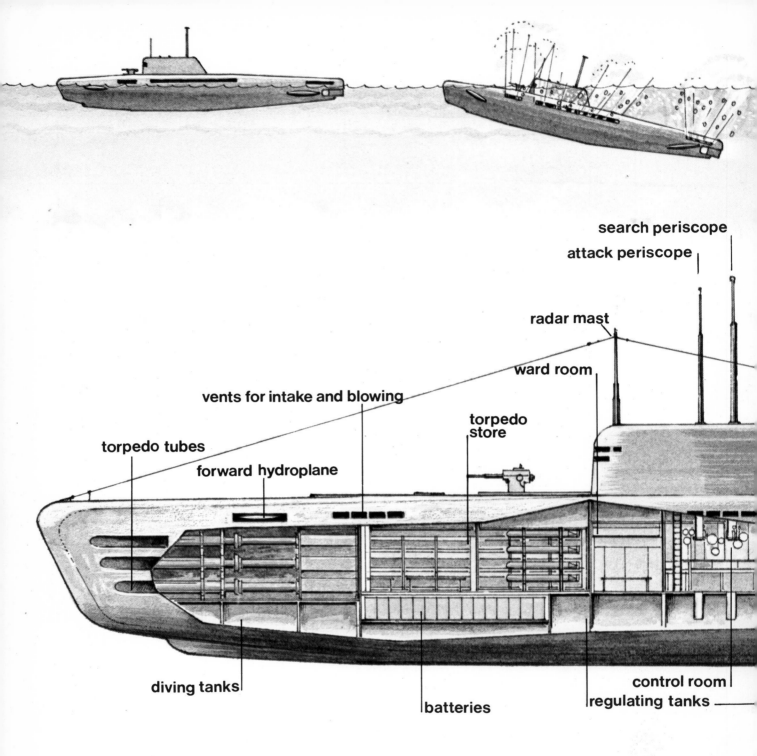

search periscope

attack periscope

radar mast

ward room

vents for intake and blowing

torpedo store

torpedo tubes

forward hydroplane

diving tanks

batteries

control room

regulating tanks

How Submarines Operate

Submarines, like all ships, depend on buoyancy to stay afloat. A series of tanks are fitted to all submarines. When flooded with water they give the ship a negative buoyancy and it begins to sink. At a desired depth, pumps or compressed air clear the water out of the tanks until a neutral buoyancy is achieved. The submarines will then float at the desired depth. To surface, the tanks are blown empty to give the ship a positive buoyancy.

All submarines depend for their ability to dive upon changing their buoyancy. They are equipped with thick inner pressure hulls and lighter outer hulls. The space between the hulls is divided into several diving and trim tanks. The diving tanks control the depth at which a submarine will ride and the trim tanks are used to keep the ship steady on an even level and at a neutral buoyancy.

But diving tanks alone are insufficient to

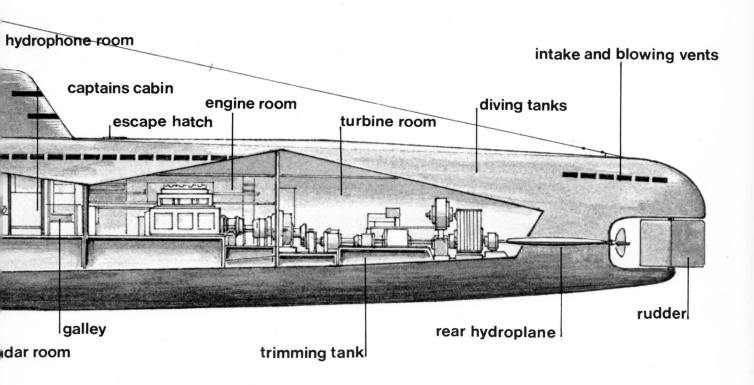

snorkel

hydrophone room

intake and blowing vents

captains cabin

engine room

diving tanks

escape hatch

turbine room

radar room

galley

trimming tank

rear hydroplane

rudder

manoeuvre a submarine. Some form of propeller is essential to drive it forward. Rudders are also necessary to steer the ship to the left or right and diving planes are usually attached to help control the angle of a dive. The planes are short, stubby wings which can be tilted to force the submarine up or down. The interaction of the tanks, propeller and diving planes are used to achieve a perfect balance in every variety of submarine vessel.

Top: The submarine dives (on the right) by flooding its tanks with water (arrowed). This increases its weight. To surface, the submarine blows the water out of its tanks and increases its buoyancy once more. By taking in more or less water and by achieving a balance of air and water in its tanks, the submarine can hold itself at any depth under the surface. The stubby hydroplanes give added control over the angle of dive, by being tilted so as to force the submarine up or down more rapidly. Above: A cut-away section of a typical submarine, showing the main working parts. These war machines posed a threat from a new angle – an unseen enemy.

The Birth of the Modern Submarine

The late 19th Century saw the predominance of sail gave way to the steam, and later the diesel, engine. These advances in mechanical propulsion soon led to efforts to install engines in submarines as well as other warships. At first, these attempts met with little success since the heat of a steam engine's furnace and its ponderous bulk made it totally impractical in an underwater ship. However, with the invention of electric engines powered by a system of batteries, a practical power plant was found.

In 1886, two Englishmen, Andrew Campbell and James Ash, designed the first electrically driven submarine, the *Nautilus*. It had a speed of six to eight knots and a range of 80 miles. But electric engines of this type had a severe drawback. Unless their batteries could be readily recharged, a submarine of this kind would be marooned without alternative power once it had cruised its maximum range.

The first submarine to overcome the limitations of the electric engine was designed and built by J. P. Holland in the late 1890s. Holland, working in America, took one of the newly developed automobile petrol engines, combined it with an electric motor and produced a power plant suitable for both underwater and long-distance surface cruising. Running on the surface with its hatches open, the ship was driven by the petrol engine. At the same time, the engine ran a generator that recharged the batteries. Once submerged, the electric engine took over the propulsion of the ship until the batteries were exhausted. The first *Holland* submarine to be produced was accepted by the U.S. Navy in 1900. It displaced close to 75 tons and had a length of 54 feet. Its cruising range was 1,500 miles, travelling at seven knots on the surface and six knots submerged.

At the same time that Holland was perfecting his invention another American, named Simon Lake, was working on the problem of a submarine's manoeuvrability. Through trial and error he finally came up with a periscope which

The Nautilus *was the first electrically driven sub. The Admiralty took a poor view of it when Sir William White, Director o*

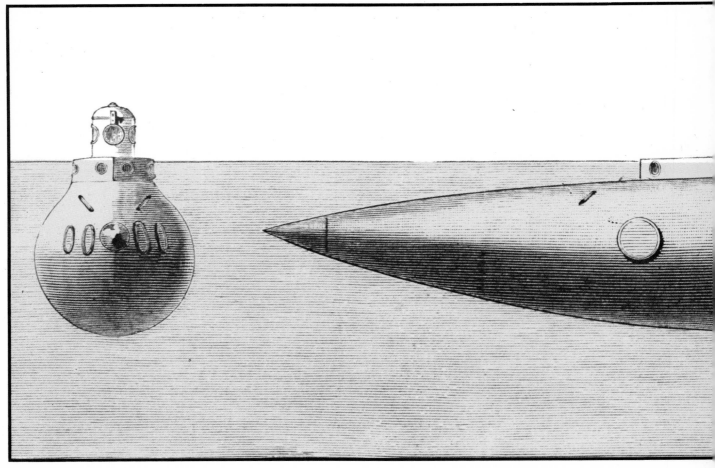

could be used when submerged. Instead of running blind when underwater, a submarine could have a wide-angle view of the surface as well as a magnified image of it. Although a periscope had a very limited horizon, its slender silhouette poking above the surface was difficult to spot from a ship's bridge. The submarine became an effective, nearly invisible hunter.

By the nature of their design, the early petrol engines were dirty and dangerous to run. The volatile engine fumes could never be vented entirely from the submarine. In the cramped enclosure of the ship's hull, the danger of a shattering explosion was ever present. The solution was found in an engine built in the 1890s and named after its German inventor, Rudolph Diesel. Diesel engines burned a fuel oil that was far less volatile then gasoline. They were cheaper to run and more efficient in their fuel consump- had successfully launched the first diesel-electric powered submarine.

Although research and development had pro-

duced an underwater boat capable of long distance travelling and submerged manoeuvring, without any armament it was little more than a transport and reconnaissance vessel. Even fitted with a deck gun a surfaced submarine could never hold its own against a conventional warship. It was the invention of the Whitehead torpedo, in 1868, that introduced a weapon whose potential was well suited to the submarine. Early torpedoes ran just below the surface on compressed air and had a limited range of only several hundred yards. A Swede, Torsten Nordenfelt, was the first to fit torpedo tubes inside the hull of a submarine. The tubes could be loaded from inside and the torpedoes launched while the submarine was totally submerged. By the First World War, torpedoes had been fitted with electric motors and stubby vanes to control their running depths, and could travel seven to eight thousand yards at speeds of 36 knots and deliver a 500 pound charge of TNT. The *Holland* submarine was the first to make use of torpedoes.

Naval Construction, was stuck in it at the bottom of the Thames on its test run.

The Total Underwater Weapon

Fitted with a periscope, a diesel-electric power plant, and armed with torpedoes and four- to five-inch deck guns, the submarine became a fearsome weapon. Travelling 17.5 knots on the surface and seven knots submerged, the long-range 'Unterseeboote', or U-boat, that Germany put to sea in the First World War, was a weapon fit to challenge the mightiest of conventional warships. In September, 1914, the German *U-9* sank three British cruisers steaming off the Dutch coast in slightly over 90 minutes. In the following four years more than 11,000,000 tons of Allied shipping, about 2,500 vessels in all, were sent to the bottom.

The only flaw which kept submarines from being used as fully submersible ships was the need to surface when running the generators that recharged the batteries. This limitation meant that submarines could only function as diving torpedo ships. None could operate beneath the waves for longer than 48 hours. Running the diesel engine and generators was a surface operation which revealed a submarine's course to reconnaissance aeroplanes and made it a vulnerable target to warships. The *schnorkel* was Germany's answer to the problem. Copying a Dutch design of 1938, they attached a pair of airpipes to the conning tower. One pipe sucked in air for the engine and crew, while the second operated as an engine exhaust. Valves in the pipes kept seawater from entering. In the course of the Second World War, German submarines were fitted with schnorkels, enabling them to breathe while at depths of up to 30 feet.

*U35 surfaces in the Mediterranean in 1917.
The U35 was the record breaking submarine of the
First World War. In a two
month period in 1916, July and August,
it sank 54 ships in the Mediterranean, almost
all by gunfire. The major
casualties were French and Italian but the
British suffered heavy losses
as well. Unrestricted submarine warfare
in the North Atlantic and the
use of torpedoes eventually led the United States
to declare war on Germany.*

The propulsion system which finally made submarines into truly underwater ships was developed by Hellmuth Walther, a German scientist. Using concentrated hydrogen peroxide as a fuel, he offered the German Navy plans for a totally self-contained turbine engine in 1937. The Walther engine operated independently of fresh air. Hydrogen peroxide was broken down chemically into water and oxygen. The oxygen was mixed with diesel oil in a combustion chamber and burned at a very high temperature. Water injected into the combustion chamber turned to high pressure steam and was drawn off with the hot gases to power a turbine unit which drove the propellers. This high-powered engine carried its own oxygen in its fuel and thus never required a source of fresh air.

Fortunately for the Allies, construction of Walther U-boats was only authorized in May, 1944. The first ships only appeared a year later; far too late to affect the course of events. They were small boats of only 850 tons but they were able to reach an underwater speed of 25 knots. None of the existing Allied anti-submarine devices would have been able to cope with a U-boat of this sort if it had appeared earlier in the war. In the last days of the war a Walther engine submarine was able to stage a dummy run on a group of British warships, coming within 500 yards – completely unnoticed.

'Happy Time' for U-Boats: the Summer of 1940

During the summer of 1940, the German 'blitz-kreig' steamrollered through Western Europe. In July, the U-boat command established its first Atlantic base at Lorient on the coast of the Bay of Biscay. This cut the length of the U-boats' old routes to the open sea by more than 400 miles, and the number of boats that could be kept in action at any one time sharply increased. At the same time, the U-boat shipyards were moving into high gear and were easily able to replace combat losses.

The lessons of the First World War had been well learned by such commanders as Karl Dönitz, admiral of the U-boat fleet. He remembered the constant frustrations of foiled daytime attacks. Time and again, his boats were spotted on the surface and obliged to submerge and run. He devised new tactics of shadowing convoys during the day and attacking only at night. This way his U-boats could approach with impunity, their low silhouettes virtually invisible against the inky night waters. In turn, they were presented with the near perfect target of ships sharply etched against the light night sky. An additional advantage to this kind of attack was the speed at which a surfaced submarine could travel. Underwater, it was barely possible to attain five knots compared to 18 knots on the surface. This was faster even than some of the smaller escort ships that were herding the convoys. It permitted the submarines to creep right into the heart of a convoy and deliver repeated attacks before disappearing at high speed to a safe distance.

The use of tactics learned during the First World War and the enormous increases in manoeuvrability and endurance permitted U-boats to range far into the Atlantic, delivering attacks in all but the roughest weather. Against this well-armed foe, the out-numbered, harried Allied escorts were almost defenceless.

These were the conditions which led the German submarine captains to name the summer of 1940, 'The Happy Time'. From June to early fall, a total of 270 ships were sunk, nearly 1,400,000 tons. On the other side of the tally sheet only six U-boats were destroyed.

Under these foreboding conditions, the slow convoy SC7 prepared to sail in October, 1940. For the crossing 34 battered merchantmen gathered in Sydney, Nova Scotia. These under-powered, overladen ships could barely manage seven knots in the best of conditions. The lightly armed sloop, Scarborough, was the only escort protection the convoy had until a Western Approaches force could rendezvous with them.

The fourth day from Sydney, a gale sprang up which separated four unwieldy Great Lakes steamers from the main body of ships. Three of them were sunk by U-boats prowling for stragglers. On the eleventh day, two more escorts joined convoy SC7. They were the Fowey, a sister sloop of the Scarborough, and the Bluebell, one of the newly commissioned Flower class corvettes. With the escorts positioned ahead, astern and to the starboard, the convoy proceeded on its way.

A distance of at least five miles separated each of the three escorts, forming a defensive screen so widely spaced that any surfaced U-boat could easily penetrate the convoy's centre. The first U-boat to spot the convoy, U-48, radioed its course and speed and brought six other submarines hurrying to intercept. Then moving in to attack it fired a round of torpedoes, scoring two hits. The attack brought the three escorts hurrying to the sinking ships. While one picked up survivors, the other two crisscrossed the area hunting with their asdic units. Although this tactic left the convoy defenceless, U-48 had been forced to submerge and break off all contact. The escorts' response revealed a fatal lack of planning. Not having worked out a cohesive defence and being over-eager to counter-attack the U-boats, they often left the convoy without any protection whatsoever. Under a sustained wolfpack attack, the convoy's protection would be a shambles.

The convoy managed to shake off U-48 but

Death of a merchantman as a U-boat claims another victim.

the following evening a solitary submarine, *U-38*, penetrated the escort screen and torpedoed a freighter. At the same time, the U-boat pinpointed the convoy's position and was able to call in the approaching wolfpack. That evening two additional escorts, the sloop *Leith* and the corvette *Heartsease*, joined convoy SC7. The *Scarborough*, meanwhile, had fallen so far behind in a vain search to hunt down a sighted submarine that it failed to rejoin the convoy for the crucial battle that was approaching.

The following evening the convoy sailed into the ambush of the waiting submarine pack. A Swedish ship was the first to be hit. The *Leith* and *Fowey* rushed to pick up the survivors and to conduct a search sweep. Once again, the convoy was left with virtually no effective escort. The attacking submarines swept in, roaming through the columns of ships at will. Torpedo after torpedo rammed into the merchantmen, crippling or sinking them. In the confusion, the risk of collision drove the remaining ships to break formation entirely.

The escorts were desperately overworked, picking up crews from the water, hunting for the attacking U-boats and herding the remaining ships into some form of order. The lack of a systematic plan of defence made their task impossible. Ship after ship was hit and yet the escorts were unable to strike back and halt the continuous attack.

Dawn found the convoy totally scattered. The *Fowey* was able to round up eight ships that day but driving rain the following night scattered them again. By now, the surviving ships were well within the channel between Ireland and Britain. Here, aircover made the U-boats reluctant to follow and few, in any case, had sufficient torpedoes left to continue the attack. The remaining ships finally made their way to port. Of the 34 ships that had sailed from Sydney, 20 were sunk and two damaged. During the final battle only one submarine had been sighted and even that had been able to escape. The U-boats held the initiative throughout the entire engagement. Had their success continued, the British war effort would have come to a halt.

After the war, Britain experimented with two Walther-engine submarines. Although they performed excellently, the launching of the first atomic-powered submarine in 1955, the U.S.S. *Nautilus*, made them obsolete. The United States began to build a fleet of nuclear submarines that revolutionized naval warfare.

Above: The SS Kemmendine, *sunk in June, 1941.*

Bottom left: A U-boat captain in his conning tower. Below: A U-boat gun crew in action.

BREAKTHROUGH ON THE POWDER FRONT

We must now turn back and follow the major breakthroughs in other areas of maritime warfare. Although speculation towards the end of the 19th Century suggested that the major role in sea warfare would be usurped by the torpedo, armaments and battleships underwent further development, thus reasserting their prime importance.

The first breakthrough came with the manufacture of slow-burning large grain powder (called prismatic powder) which gave guns a much greater muzzle velocity. The aim of the new powder was to prolong the charge on the missile for as long as possible. It was later discovered that if the gun was *chambered* (that is, making the powder chamber larger than the charge) a greater amount of slow burning powder could be used without increasing the maximum pressure on the gun casing. It was soon found, however, that the shell left the barrel before the charge was completely consumed. Longer muzzles proved the solution to that particular problem but the lengthened muzzle made muzzle-loading a problem. The alternative was to switch to breech-loading mechanisms.

Breech-loaders had been overlooked in the British navy because of the fact that the guns could possibly be fired without the breech being properly closed, a dangerous hazard to both gunners and ship. The French and Germans had perfected breech-loading mechanisms, using automatic safety devices to ensure against

The Mercury *was one of the first all-steel-hulled cruisers in the Royal Navy.*

accidents. The French adapted an American design for an interrupted-screw breech block which was introduced into the French navy in 1858. The breech block was divided into four sections of interrupted screw threads. The operating lever swung the block into the breech, rotating it so that the screw threads engaged, thus locking the mechanism in place. The Germans used an improved Armstrong wedge system to achieve the same effect.

The universal adoption of breech-loading mechanisms left guns free to develop as large as they could within the confines of existing warships. Slower-burning powders were invented to take full advantage of increased barrel length. Prismatic powder became 'cocoa' powder which in turn was replaced by cordite. Cordite was a smokeless powder made up of guncotton and nitroglycerine. It was a much more powerful explosive agent than ordinary gun powder and made possible the development of larger guns capable of quicker fire.

The introduction of more efficient ordnance led, as usual, to changes in armour. But the usual response of thicker armour could no longer apply. There was a limit to the weight of armour a ship could carry. A new kind of armour was needed, not just more of the same. The eventual solution was the use of steel. In the late 1870s steel was introduced in the cruisers *Iris* and *Mercury*, making them the first all-steel hulled ships in the Royal Navy.

HMS Majestic *showing the interior of the barbette or gun turret.*

The Crucial Factors at Tsushima

For well over a generation a seemingly endless flow of technological innovations gave promise of stronger and more destructive navies. The transformation of the sailing man-of-war to the iron (later steel) hulled modern battleship was completed by the 1870s. The broadside had given way to the revolving turret, the small smooth bore cannon to the big guns with their greater speed, accuracy and hitting power. But no matter what the theoreticians said or what the reports of naval manoeuvres indicated the real test remained battle on the high seas. It was with great interest, therefore, that the naval powers of the world studied the Battle of Tsushima during the Russo-Japanese war of 1904–5. This battle, as one historian put it, 'was the first (and also last) occasion when opposing lines of ironclads joined battle and fought to a finish in the way naval theory prescribed'.

From being a backward, feudal nation, sub-servient to the gunboat diplomacy of European and American powers, Japan had in the short space of 50 years become the most powerful Asian country and was well on her way to being one of the world's great powers. She had shown

Russian ship breaks Japanese blockade at Port Arthur.

herself a willing and able student of the Western-ers whom she had loathed so much. By 1904 she was ready to show the results of her studies.

The Russo-Japanese war was a contest between two imperialist countries squabbling over shares of the dismembered China. In February, 1904, without a formal declaration of war, Japan swooped down on the Russian ships anchored in Port Arthur, using the much-touted torpedo

boats. The torpedo, due to its small range and great inaccuracy, proved to be a much less formidable weapon than had been claimed by the protagonists. Further action around Port Arthur showed that the great and medium range quick-firing gun shooting from some distance was to be the decisive element in combat.

By the spring of 1904 the Russian Eastern fleet had been destroyed by the Japanese. In a

A Russian battleship is towed into captivity. Speed and accurate gunnery shattered the Russian navy at Tsushima.

desperate attempt to curtail his Far Eastern losses the Russian Czar, Nicholas II, ordered his Baltic fleet to the Sea of Japan. 'The Japanese must be put in their place,' Rozhdestvensky was told. The 56-year-old Rozhdestvensky was a brave man but he had last seen action years before in the Turkish campaigns. The Baltic fleet was a disparate collection of five modern and three old battleships, three coastal defence ships and an old armoured cruiser. It would take an experienced admiral to weld that motley collection into an effective fighting forcé. Alas, Admiral Rozhdestvensky had neither the necessary experience nor had he the capabilities of a really good commander.

Admiral Togo on the other hand already had the destruction of the Russian Eastern fleet to his credit. He also had ample time to prepare for the next and final stage of the war while Rozhdestvensky continued on his laborious way round the Cape of Good Hope.

Sixteen months after the opening of hostilities the Baltic fleet arrived in the Sea of Japan. Rozhestvensky formed his fleet into two columns hoping to force a passage through the straits of Tsushima to Vladivostock. Rozhdestvensky led the stronger, starboard line in his flagship, the *Suvaroff*. Nebogatoff commanded the port line of eight ships. Three fast cruisers formed a vanguard while two cruisers and four destroyers held the rear. These were followed by the supply and hospital ships.

Togo's tactics were simple. The Russians had the superiority in heavy guns but he had the advantage in speed. Therefore his big battleships would cut off the Russian advance while the cruisers would circle around the Russian line and take it from the rear. The battle began just after 2 p.m. on May 27. Everything seemed to follow the book. Togo chose his range at about 9,500 yards and opened fire on Rozhdestvensky's column. Within an hour the *Suvaroff* was disabled, her flag-captain killed and the Admiral himself wounded twice. The speed of the Japanese boats and the accuracy of their fire left no doubt as to the outcome of the battle. The Russian were ill-prepared, a high proportion of their shells failed to explode and their gunnery collapsed after the initial Japanese onslaught.

As night fell the surviving Russian ships hoped to escape to Vladivostock but even this was not allowed them. Togo wanted a complete victory. The torpedo boats were sent in and completed the devastation wrought by the battleships and cruisers. The Russian fleet was completely annihilated. Fourteen battleships and five armoured cruisers were lost. Only one small cruiser and two destroyers reached Vladivostock. From a potentially great naval power, Russia was reduced overnight to a third class naval force.

Tsushima taught the navies of the world that guns and speed were the crucial factors in a naval engagement. Superior gunnery, the use of high explosive shells, and the speed of the armoured cruisers were the important factors in the Japanese victory. The much-vaunted torpedo boat was seen in its true perspective – an important auxiliary weapon, not the dominant factor in naval warfare. Henceforth the naval powers of the world concentrated on the development of the big gun battleship.

The Russians had the superiority in heavy firepower but the Japanese navy had a distinct edge when it came to speed. The Japanese also displayed considerably greater firing accuracy.

Below: The Russian Baltic fleet. On the left is Rozhdestvensky's flagship, the Suvaroff.

DREADNOUGHT OR DINOSAUR?

The Dreadnought ship was the greatest development of the battleship but, unfortunately, in many ways it resembled the dinosaur – too big for its own good.

As early as 1903 an Italian engineer, Cuniberti, wrote an article arguing for a big gun warship which would be armed with 12 12-inch guns and which would have a speed superior to any contemporary battleship. At the time Cuniberti's proposals were quite revolutionary and raised a great deal of resistance in naval quarters. It was felt, and quite rightly too, that the development of such a ship would render obsolete all preceding classes of warships.

Yet three years later King Edward VII launched the *Dreadnought*. The outstanding features of the *Dreadnought* were the 10 12-inch guns mounted in five turrets: one facing fore, two aft, and one on each side just forward of amidships. The positioning of the turrets enabled six guns to be fired forward and a possible eight guns fired in broadside.

Of the 27 12-pound guns, 12 were mounted on the superstructure, 2 on each turret top, and 2 on the quarter-deck. These guns were to be used as a counter-offensive against torpedo boats and destroyers. The *Dreadnought* was plated with an armour of 11-inch toughened mild steel below

HMS Dreadnought.

the waterline with a belt of eight-inch plating just above it. The bow and the stem were protected by six-inch and four-inch armour respectively.

The *Dreadnought* was the first large battleship to be fitted with a turbine engine, giving her a maximum speed of 21 knots. She was the most efficient ship in the world in her time, for the turbine engines dispensed with the time-consuming and laborious process of overhauling the engines, so necessary with the old steam engines even after a single day's steaming at high speed. She also made use of wireless.

This revolutionary battleship gave her name to a new world-wide class of warships. Not only

was she bigger than anything that had been built previously, she was stronger and was capable of engaging two and a half of the older warships on an equal basis. Indeed the Germans soon referred to the pre-dreadnoughts as 'funf-minuten' ships – able to survive for only five minutes under the terrible firepower of the all-powerful dreadnought.

It can be seen, therefore, why it was that the British launched the dreadnought programme with some trepidation. Her undoubted naval superiority was put in jeopardy, for the Germans could commence to build their own dreadnoughts and maintain an even pace with the British.

BATTLECRUISERS AT SPEED

Speed and firepower were the two important factors in naval warfare. The dreadnoughts accounted for firepower and the battlecruisers were developed at about the same time for speed.

In aim the battlecruiser was the descendant of the sailing frigate: that is, the eye of the fleet. The design was directed towards producing a ship of superior speed, enabling her to reconnoitre in the face of the enemy. The British launched the first battlecruisers in 1907 – the *Indomitable*, *Inflexible* and *Invincible*. Of necessity speed meant a sacrifice in heavy-weight armour and armament. The battlecruisers were constructed with a medium armour seven inches thick but their firing power was kept nearly equal to ships of the dreadnought class. For, by lightening the ship in other respects, eight 12-inch guns could be retained. These 12-inch guns were mounted two to a turret with two turrets along the centre-line, fore and aft, and one each side. She also carried 16 four-inch guns able to fire 12 times a minute, and five submerged torpedo tubes placed in the bow and stern. The cruiser was also fitted with two anti-aircraft guns (A.A. guns), which were introduced owing to the success of early experiments with 'heavier than air' flying machines. The battlecruiser had an indicated horsepower of 41,000 (18,000 for the *Dreadnought*) and attained a maximum speed of 26 knots.

Speed and Firepower Decide Battle of Coronel and Falkland Islands

As with the dreadnoughts the Germans were quick to follow the British lead. They swiftly built up a fleet of battlecruisers which proved cruelly effective in the early years of the First World War. The battlecruiser was ideal for the tasks the Germans gave them – quick hit-and-run raids on merchant shipping and unprotected ports and harbours. As Vice-Admiral Graf Maximilian von Spee wrote, 'A single light cruiser can coal from captured vessels and maintain herself for longer . . . as there are great prizes to be won there, I despatched the fastest light cruiser.' Spee had just given permission for the *Emden* to operate raids in the Indian Ocean. For two months, through September and October of 1914, the *Emden* conducted devastating raids on allied shipping. Nine ships were sunk in September, a Russian cruiser and a French destroyer were sunk in Penang harbour in October. But then her luck ran out. In an attempted raid on the Cocos Islands she ran into

Top: HMS Inflexible. *Above:* HMS Indomitable *at full spee*
Right: HMS Invincible. *These three were*
the first British battlecruisers (1907), descendants of
the frigate and used as the eyes of the fleet.

a heavily escorted Anzac convoy. Captain Glossop of H.M.A.S. *Sydney* was despatched to pursue the bold raider. After a long running battle he managed to run her to ground on the coral reefs off the islands.

Meanwhile the rest of von Spee's squadron had been operating in the Pacific, off the Chilean coast. The British High Command feared he would begin raiding operations on the trade routes in the Atlantic. The Admiralty ordered Rear-Admiral Craddock to the Falkland Islands with the command to 'get Spee.' At Craddock's disposal were the old armoured cruiser *Monmouth*, the modern light cruiser *Glasgow*, and the armed merchantman *Otranto*. Craddock's flagship was the armoured cruiser *Good Hope*. Also present was the old battleship *Canopus*. The search for the German raider began.

Spee commanded two heavy cruisers, the *Scharnhorst* and *Gneisenau* and three light cruisers, the *Nürnberg*, the *Leipzig* and the *Dresden*. The German ships were faster and more powerful than the punitive British force.

Upon learning the nature of his opponents, Spee set off immediately to seek a confrontation. On Sunday November 1, 1914, the Germans espied the British ships off Coronel. By six in the evening the battle lines were formed and at 7.04 the Germans opened fire at a range of 12,000 yards. The *Scharnhorst* and *Gneisenau* concentrated their fire on the *Good Hope* and the *Monmouth*. The German shells found their mark and the *Good Hope* was disastrously hit; her foredeck exploded, burning brilliantly in the dark night. The brightly lit *Good Hope* provided an excellent target for the German gunners who were themselves sheathed in darkness.

The only hope for the British now lay in closing the range. Craddock led his ships towards the German line but Spee was too fast and kept the

Above: The German armoured cruiser Gneisenau. *Weight: 11,600 tons; speed: 22·5 knots; armament: eight 8·2 in guns.*

Above: The Gneisenau's *sister ship, the* Scharnhorst.

range to his own advantage. In a last desperate attempt to gain satisfaction from the enemy, Craddock charged the *Scharnhorst*. The heavy German ships turned their broadsides on the ill-fated cruiser, subjecting her to a ferocious barrage from which there was no escape. The *Good Hope* exploded and sank with all hands on board. A similar fate awaited the *Monmouth* at the hands of the *Nürnberg*. Only the *Otranto* and the *Glasgow* managed to escape.

News of the defeat at Coronel shocked the Admiralty into action. The *Invincible* and *Inflexible*, as superior to the German vessels as they had been to the *Good Hope* and the *Monmouth*, were sent to accomplish what Craddock with his inferior ships could not, the complete destruction of Spee's squadron.

On December 7, 1914, Vice-Admiral Sir Frederick Doveton Sturdee arrived at Port Stanley in the Falkland Islands. In addition to the two battlecruisers he had with him six cruisers and an armed merchantman. There was no doubt that with his superior force Sturdee

*Left:
Von Spee,
dreaded raider
of the Pacific. Right: Sir Doveton Sturdee.
He finally put paid to Von Spee's activities.*

The Inflexible *and* Invincible *chase Von Spee's squadron at the Battle of the Falkland Isles.*

would defeat the Germans. The problem was to find them. Luck was with the British, for the day after their arrival at Port Stanley Sturdee received the news that *Gneisenau* and *Nürnberg* were steaming towards the port followed by the rest of Spee's ships.

In choosing to attack the Falkland Islands Spee made the critical error of his career. Why he chose to do so is not known but it is certain that if he had ordered an immediate attack he could have inflicted serious damage on the unprepared British fleet, although at the cost of his own ships. As it was, when informed of the presence of the British warships Spee gave the order: 'Do not accept action. Concentrate on course east by south. Proceed at full speed.'

Sturdee gave chase and the first shots of the Battle of the Falkland Islands were fired just before one in the afternoon. Seeing that he was outnumbered, Spee ordered his light cruisers to slip away, hoping to hold the British with his armoured cruisers. The British cruisers gave chase while the *Invincible* and the *Inflexible*

concentrated their fire on the *Gneisenau* and the *Scharnhorst*. Just as the German ships had pounded the *Good Hope* and the *Monmouth* into the sea so now the *Invincible* and *Inflexible* savagely mauled the *Scharnhorst* and the *Gneisenau*. Twist and turn as they might, the German vessels could not escape the inexorable fire power of the British. By five in the afternoon the battle was over. The two German cruisers had been sunk; of the light cruisers the *Nürnberg* and *Leipzig* suffered the same fate that night and the *Dresden* was captured four days later.

The lesson of Coronel and the Falkland Islands battles was clear: no matter how brilliant the commander, it was not possible to send an inferior fleet to face a more powerful enemy and hope to win. The *Scharnhorst* and the *Gneisenau* outclassed Craddock's vessels and were easily able to destroy them; the *Invincible* and *Inflexible* greatly outclassed the German armoured cruisers and annihilated them in face-to-face combat. In each case speed and firepower were the important elements leading to victory.

Jutland: The Clash of the Leviathan

Coronel and the Falkland Islands were diversionary engagements. The main British and German forces of dreadnoughts and battle-cruisers lay waiting apprehensively to the north in the North Sea. Both sides were eager to test the might of their naval arms but, wary of head-on conflict, sought to engage the enemy by means of various traps.

The German fleet, commanded by Vice Admiral Scheer, could not attack the whole British fleet owing to its numerical inferiority. The alternative was to trap part of it, probably the battle-cruiser force, and engage before the larger battleship complement could intervene.

With this end in mind Scheer settled upon two plans. The first was to mount an attack on one of Britain's east coast ports, Sunderland, using Vice-Admiral Hipper's battlecruiser fleet. Submarines and the main battle force under Scheer's personal command would cover for Hipper.

The second and similar plan was to have Hipper raid British shipping steaming off the nearby Danish coasts. Again the submarines and Scheer's battleships would stay hidden, to emerge

The Indefatigable *steaming into battle at Jutland.*

at the crucial moment of battle.

Scheer hoped to put the first plan into operation but bad weather made it inadvisable and on May 30, 1916, he ordered Hipper's cruiser force to make an appearance off the Norwegian coast. Scheer thus thought to lure an investigating enemy fleet into his trap.

The British Admiralty were well aware, however, that the Germans were up to something. The British had decoded the German's secret message and were kept well-informed of impending moves. Admiral Sir John Jellicoe, stationed at Scapa Flow in the Orkney Islands, was ordered south. Vice-Admiral Beatty led a vanguard force of six battlecruisers escorted by cruisers and destroyers.

The first phase of the Battle of Jutland, the South Run, saw Beatty dash towards Hipper's fleet, guns blazing. Hipper, meanwhile, drew back leading Beatty towards Scheer. The battlecruiser duel went badly for the British. Three of Beatty's ships were badly hit before he scored a return hit against the Germans. Fortunately a fast battleship force under Evan-Thomas appeared within

range. The heavy 15-inch guns bombarded the enemy fleet, forcing Hipper to retreat. At about the same time (4.30 in the afternoon) Scheer's main battleship force hove into sight. Hipper was saved but the delighted British could now hope to bring the full weight of their naval might on the Germans and finally, irrevocably crush them into defeat.

The second phase of the battle saw a complete turnabout on the first. Beatty drew the enemy after him, leading them towards the main British fleet in the north.

Unaware of the trap awaiting him, Scheer was jubilant at the thought of victory over such a redoubtable adversary. He congratulated himself on his clever plans and looked forward to the accolades of the Kaiser. Great was his surprise when out of the smoke and haze he saw looming ahead of him the massed might of the British fleet. The horizon from the north to east was a sea of fire; destruction seemed certain. His only possible move was a complete about face which he immediately ordered. He still, however, had to make his way back to base. Several times

Above: A rare photograph of the Battle of Jutland taken from a British destroyer engaged in the action. Below: The König Albert, *one of Scheer's battleships.*

Artist Norman Howard's impression of the Battle of Jutland. To the left are the British, on the right the Germans.

during the late afternoon Scheer changed course, always managing to avoid Jellicoe's fleet. To gain valuable time he ordered Hipper's cruisers back into the fray. The battleships must be saved at all costs, reasoned Scheer, even if it meant the sacrifice of the cruisers.

Night fell and Scheer knew that either he must get past the British fleet or else face utter ruin on the morrow. Three choices of route lay before him. He could head south-west towards the River Ems, south-east towards the Horn Reef and the River Elbe, or south to Heligoland and Wilhelmshaven.

Jellicoe decided that the Germans would choose the southerly route despite advice that the Horn Reef route was more likely. He did, however, despatch a minelayer to block the Horn Reef channel. Jellicoe's plan was to cut off Scheer's route into the German Bight. And even if Scheer took the Horn Reef route he would have to pass astern of Jellicoe's battle squadrons and Jellicoe could count on the flotilla to keep him informed of Scheer's position. As it turned out the flotilla did nothing of the sort. Scheer slipped past the British fleet and by daylight was safe. Thus ended in anticlimax what was to be

the greatest naval engagement of the war.

Years of controversy, massive armaments build-up, and anxious expectation led up to the Battle of Jutland. At last, it was felt, the dreadnought would be put to the test. The results were inconclusive, to say the least. The British lost three capital ships, three cruisers, and a few destroyers; the Germans lost one battlecruiser, four cruisers, a pre-dreadnought battleship, and some destroyers, though many of the other German ships were severely mauled. Both sides claimed victory and even 60 years later debate rages as to who in fact won. One outcome of the

battle was the Kaiser's decision not to risk his fleet again in dangerous ventures. Once again he ordered the submarines to take the offensive, thus bringing the United States into the war.

The big gun battleship never had a chance to display its combat virtuosity and it was not long before the days of the dreadnought were numbered. 'Never again,' wrote one historian, 'would long lines of the steel clad leviathans move ponderously into action and prepare to fight it out in an exchange of shell fire.' The whole nature of naval warfare was changed by the submarine and the availability of aircraft.

THE WASHINGTON TREATY: A LIMIT TO POWER

After the end of the First World War there was a virtual halt in ship construction. Naval power shifted from Europe to America and Japan. After the war the Japanese announced that they were about to build a fleet of eight battleships and eight cruisers, none of which was to undergo more than eight years of service. The Americans took this as a challenge and commenced a building programme of ten battleships and six cruisers. Due to the Washington Treaty of 1921 the Americans only completed two of their battleships – the *Colorado* and the *West Virginia*. Displacing 32,000 tons and armed with eight 16-inch guns, the two ships were also fitted with the new turbo-electric engines. The turbo-electric engine differed from the conventional steam turbine by having the propeller shaft driven by an electric motor. The turbo-electric engine added to the efficiency and speed of the newly constructed battleships.

The trend towards bigger gun battleships was cut short in late 1921 by a conference called by the United States government to discuss a limitation on naval armaments. The United States, Britain, Japan, Italy, and France signed a treaty limiting their capital ship tonnage to a proportion of 5:5:3:1l75:1·75 respectively. They also agreed not to build or acquire any new ships except in replacement of those lost or upon reaching 20 years of age. In addition any new ships built would not exceed 35,000 tons displacement.

The first ships to be built to these standards were the British battleships *Nelson* and *Rodney*. Their main armament consisted of nine 16-inch guns mounted in three turrets, two fore and one aft, with a secondary armament of 12 6-inch guns mounted in two power-worked turrets. Apart from abandonment of all-round armour protection, these ships saved valuable weight by the introduction of super-heated steam, reducing the number of boilers to eight.

The design of the armoured cruiser was also constricted by the terms of the Washington Treaty. The cruiser was limited to a maximum displacement of 10,000 tons and to armament not exceeding eight inches calibre.

The effect on cruiser construction was the attempt to squeeze as many eight-inch guns as possible on the reduced cruiser with all thoughts of armour protection thrown out the window.

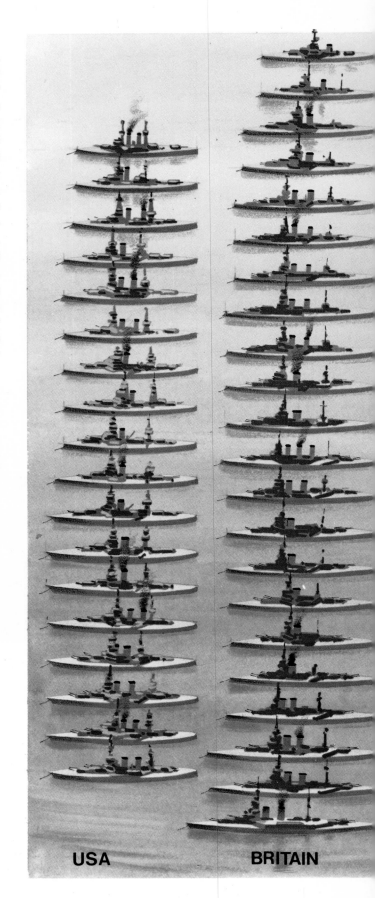

USA

BRITAIN

In 1924: relative naval strengths of the five signatories, 2½ years after signing the Washington Treaty.

USA	BRITAIN	FRANCE	ITALY	JAPAN
	Thunderer			
	King George V			
	Ajax			
	Centurion			
Utah	Iron Duke			
Florida	Marlborough			
Wyoming	Emperor of India			
Arkansas	Benbow			
New York	Barham			
Texas	Warspite			
Nevada	Queen Elizabeth			
Oklahoma	Tiger			
Arizona	Malaya			Kongo
Pennsylvania	Royal Sovereign	Voltaire		Hiyei
Mississipi	Resolution	Diderot		Haruna
New Mexico	Revenge	Condorcet	Napoli	Hirishima
Idaho	Royal Oak	Courbet	Roma	Fuso
Tennessee	Ramillies	Jean Bart	Dante Alighieri	Yamashiro
California	Valliant	Paris	Guilio Cesare	Ise
Maryland	Repulse	Provence	Conte di Cavour	Hiuga
Colorado	Renown	Bretagne	Caio Duilio	Nagato
West Virginia	Hood	Lorraine	Andrea Doria	Mutsu

FRANCE   **ITALY**   **JAPAN**

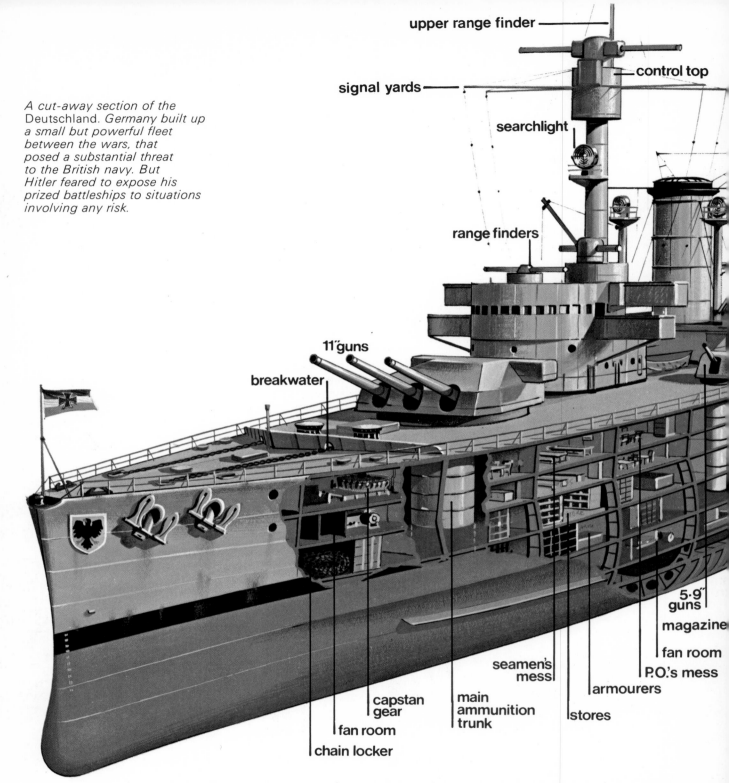

upper range finder

control top

signal yards

searchlight

range finders

A cut-away section of the Deutschland. Germany built up a small but powerful fleet between the wars, that posed a substantial threat to the British navy. But Hitler feared to expose his prized battleships to situations involving any risk.

11˝ guns

breakwater

5·9˝ guns

magazine

fan room

P.O.'s mess

seamen's mess

armourers

capstan gear

main ammunition trunk

stores

fan room

chain locker

The most interesting and revolutionary designs were those of the Germans, whose ships came to be know as pocket battleships. Building ships of 12,000 tons displacement, the Germans armed them with six 11-inch guns and a mixed secondary armament of 5·9- and 4·1-inch guns as well as eight torpedo tubes. Diesel engines developing 56,000 horsepower gave these ships a speed of up to 26 knots, making them formidable commerce-raiders.

Later the Germans created the first all-welded ship. It replaced the standard riveting process of making the ships stronger and lighter.

The Washington Treaty expired in 1930 but was renewed as the London Naval Treaty. The latter treaty was due to expire at the end of 1936 and desperate efforts were made to renew it. However, by that time international relations had become very strained. Hitler publicly denounced the Treaty of Versailles and managed to negotiate

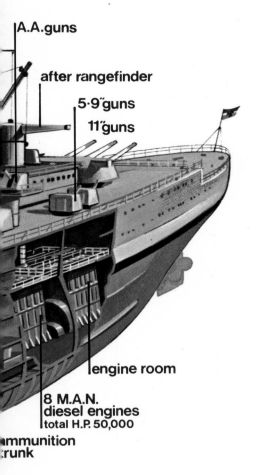

A.A.guns

after rangefinder

5·9″guns

11″guns

engine room

8 M.A.N.
diesel engines
total H.P. 50,000

ammunition
trunk

Top: The Yamato *carried the largest guns (18·1 ins) of any battleship in the world. Above: The* Deutschland, *one of the revolutionary German pocket battleships built in the inter-war period. An innovation in the use of welded (as opposed to riveted) hulls.*

an agreement whereby Germany could build up her naval strength to 35 per cent of that of Britain. Both Italy and Japan adopted aggressive attitudes and it was not long before the armaments race was on again.

Capital ships of great size, armour, speed, and striking power were being built, the most powerful of these by the Japanese. The *Yamato* and *Murachi*, displacing 64,170 tons, mounted nine 18·1-inch guns and maintained a top speed of 27·5 knots. However, during the Second World War the usefulness of the capital ship diminished, her role being usurped by submarines and aircraft. Battleships and cruisers alike were hurriedly equipped with greater anti-torpedo protection and high angle guns for use against aeroplanes.

The aeroplane was of paramount importance during the Second World War and its advent saw the rapid development of the aircraft carrier.

The English Atlantic Fleet in line of battle led by HMS Rodney.

THE AIRCRAFT CARRIER: A NEW DIMENSION

By the Second World War the aeroplane was without a doubt the single most powerful weapon available. The development of the aircraft carrier extended that power to the sea. Primitive aircraft carriers had been built and tested in the early years of the 20th Century. The Curtiss seaplane had aroused the interest of the United States Navy in the possibilities of aircraft. In 1910 the newly constructed *Birmingham* was made available for flight experiments. A wooden platform 83 feet long and 24 feet wide was built over the ship's bow. On November 14, a Curtiss pusher biplane was hoisted aboard and its pilot,

Eugene B. Ely, made ready for take-off. Racing the engine at full power he rolled it down the ramp. The plane dipped slightly into the water but the wooden prop held and he was airborne. It was the first successful flight of an aeroplane from a ship.

In January, 1911, Ely added another first to his collection by landing a biplane on the armoured cruiser *Pennsylvania*. Twenty-two pairs of 50-pound sandbags placed at three-foot intervals were used as arresting gear. Each pair of sandbags was connected by a line 12 inches above the deck. Three pairs of hooks were

Eugene Ely's famous landing on the U.S. cruiser Pennsylvania. *Flying at 35 mph, he was stopped within 60 ft by means of hooks on the plane which caught on to ropes on the vessel.*

attached to the aeroplane so that on landing they would catch the taut line, thus bringing the plane to a halt. Ely's hooks took hold on the 12th arresting line, stopping the biplane with a deck run of only 30 feet. Ely was greeted by the cheers of the gathered sailors and the Captain exclaimed, 'This is the most important landing of a bird since the dove flew back to the Ark.'

Developments on the other side of the Atlantic saw the birth of the first carriers. In 1912 a biplane took off from the forecastle of the British battleship *Hibernia*. A year later the French outfitted a cruiser to carry aircraft on her

Another American, Glenn Curtiss, takes off from the Birmingham *in his hydroplane — a pusher biplane with clumsy fore-and-aft structures.*

Mediterranean manoeuvres. In the same year the British adapted an old cruiser to carry two seaplanes which were launched from a short deck built forward of her bows. In 1914 an oil tanker still under construction was taken over by the Admiralty and converted to carry ten seaplanes. The *Ark Royal* had hangar space below decks and like the earlier models used cranes to hoist the planes into and out of the water.

The first true aircraft carriers were built in 1917. In that year wheeled fighter aircraft were used for the first time on a carrier. Commander F. J. Rutland flew a Sopwith Pup biplane off the deck of the *Manxman*. He proved the point that a fighter could take off on a flight deck of less than 45 feet. After Rutland's experiments orders were given for all cruisers capable of having them to be fitted with 20-foot flight decks. In March of the same year the cruiser *Furious* was completed as a partial carrier. She had a flight deck 228 feet long and 50 feet wide and supported four seaplanes and six wheeled aircraft. In November the *Furious* was overhauled and fitted with a rear landing deck 287 feet long and 70 feet wide. She now could carry 12 Sopwith Pups and eight seaplanes. In 1918 seven of her Sopwiths made history by successfully bombing the Zeppelin base at Tondern.

In 1916 the British bought the unfinished Italian liner *Conte Rosso*, rechristened her the *Argus*, and converted her into the first full-length aircraft carrier. Unencumbered by masts or funnels, she was the first flush-decked carrier, with a flight deck 550 feet long and 68 feet wide. Two elevators brought the planes up to the flight deck. The *Argus* was also the first carrier to carry torpedo aircraft but the First World War ended before their usefulness could be gauged. In 1920 the carrier *Eagle* was launched. She introduced the 'island' structure by having her mast, bridge and funnel set on the starboard side of the vessel. This allowed a great deal more landing space on the deck.

By 1925 the British navy was clearly in the lead in the development of aircraft carriers but the transfer of aviation responsibility from the Admiralty to the newly formed Royal Air Force meant that less money was spent on developing the carrier. The Americans and Japanese quickly caught up the British lead and by the Second World War were among the dominant naval powers in the world.

Early in the century Japan had sent naval officers to France and the United States to learn

Right: Official U.S. Navy photograph of Battle of Midway (June 1942) shows a Japanese heavy cruiser of the Mogami class after heavy bombardment by carrier based naval aircraft.

Below: The do's and don'ts of landing on a carrier. Many problems faced the pioneer pilots.

(a) Incorrect landing on a rolling carrier.

(b) Correct landing between rolls.

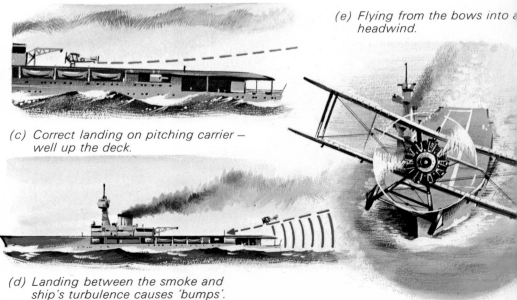

(c) Correct landing on pitching carrier — well up the deck.

(d) Landing between the smoke and ship's turbulence causes 'bumps'.

(e) Flying from the bows into a headwind.

(f) Too low an approach.

(g) The approach is too high.

(h) This is the correct approach angle.

Above: Squadron-Commander Dunning's fatal landing on the Furious.

the techniques of flying. The first Japanese Navy aeroplanes were British-bought Farman float biplanes. In 1913 the naval transport vessel *Wakamiya Maru* was refitted to carry two seaplanes. In 1919 the Japanese began construction on the second purpose-built aircraft carrier, the *Hosho* (the first was the British *Hermes*). Displacing 7,470 tons, the *Hosho* had a maximum speed of 25 knots and carried seven fighter aircraft, ten attack planes and four reconnaissance aeroplanes.

The terms of the Washington Treaty limited the United States, Britain, and Japan to two aircraft carriers. Both the United States and Japan chose to convert two of their projected capital ships. The Americans selected the semi-completed *Lexington* and *Saratoga* for conver-

sion. The completed carriers had a displacement of 36,000 tons and an armament of eight eight-inch guns and twelve five-inch anti-aircraft guns. They were 888 feet long with a huge island superstructure, and were the first carriers to incorporate flight decks and hangars as part of the main hull structure and not simply as above-hull appendages. Despite their size the *Lexington* and *Saratoga* were capable of a maximum speed of 33 knots. They were designed to carry and operate 72 aircraft.

The Japanese converted the *Akagi* and *Kaga* into carriers. The *Akagi* carried 60 aircraft, displaced 26,900 tons and could attain a speed of 32.5 knots. Her armaments consisted of ten eight-inch and 12 4·7-inch guns. The *Kaga* carried the same number of aircraft as her sister ship but

Far left: The Kaga, with its sister ship the Akagi, was one of the largest aircraft carriers in the world in 1941.

Left: A seaplane hoisted on to the Ark Royal.
Below left: The makeshift launching platform on the British battleship Hibernia (1912).
Below right: A Sopwith pup lands on HMS Furious, a cruiser converted to carrier.

was slightly smaller (783 feet as opposed to 856 feet for the *Akagi*) and slower (maximum speed 27·5 knots).

The expiration of the London Naval Treaty in 1936 enabled the Japanese to build two of her finest carriers, the *Shokaku* and the *Zuikaku*. Displacing nearly 26,000 tons, these sister ships were 846 feet long and carried 84 aircraft. They were armed with 16 five-inch guns and a great number of 25-millimetre guns. They could reach a speed of 34 knots. They were also the first carriers to carry sonar equipment.

The United States established a major class of aircraft carriers with the construction of the *Yorktown* and the *Enterprise*. Displacing just under 20,000 tons, both ships were 809 feet long. carried 80 aircraft and could move at a top speed

of 34 knots. The aircraft could be catapulted from the hangar deck as well as from the flight deck, which meant that a greater number of planes could be put into action at short notice. The main armaments of these vessels consisted of eight five-inch guns.

The Second World War saw the emerging dominance of the aircraft carrier. Each of the warring states deployed their naval vessels in task forces, the hearts of which were the carriers. The aircraft carrier was also accepted as a must for freight convoys, for they gave the necessary air cover against U-boat attacks.

Perhaps nowhere did they play a more important role than in the Pacific where a life and death struggle was raging between the powerful Japanese and American forces.

Dive-bombers at Midway

The initial Japanese onslaught saw her spreading rapidly to the south and west. Disregarding the risks of an over-extended supply line, Admiral Yamamoto wished to establish an outer defensive perimeter which would encompass the Aleutian Islands, Midway, Fiji, Samoa, New California, and Port Moresby. Stiff resistance from the United States and Australia at the Battle of the Coral Sea prevented the Japanese from taking Port Moresby. The turning point in the Pacific War came a month later at the Battle of Midway. An American aircraft carrier force halted a fearful Japanese onslaught on Midway and thus began the process of beating back the Japanese.

By May 1942 the Americans had broken the Japanese code and were aware that a major action was planned around Midway. The two carriers *Enterprise* and *Hornet* were immediately ordered to Pearl Harbour to join Admiral Fletcher's carrier, the *Yorktown*, undergoing extensive repairs. On May 30, 1942, the three carriers set out for Midway covered by eight cruisers and 14 destroyers. Rear-Admiral Spruance was placed in command of the *Enterprise* and *Hornet* while Fletcher retained command of the *Yorktown* as well as being put in charge of the overall operation.

To ensure success Yamamoto committed the full strength of the Japanese navy to the Midway assault. Eight of Japan's ten aircraft carriers, 11 battleships, 13 heavy cruisers, seven light cruisers, 68 destroyers and numerous small craft including minesweepers and supply ships formed the Japanese flotilla. The combined fleet was divided into four, with Yamamoto leading a main force of one carrier and seven battleships, Vice-Admiral Nagumo in charge of the carrier striking force, Vice-Admiral Kondo in charge of the Midway invasion force and Vice-Admiral Hosogaya leading a northern force.

Yamamoto hoped to distract American attention from Midway by bombing raids on the northern Aleutian Islands. With that accomplished, carrier bombers would devastate Midway's defences, preparing the way for the landing of the invasion force. He allowed for the U.S. Pacific Fleet by stationing submarines between the Hawaiian Islands and Midway. If necessary the carrier force would bring its strength to bear against the Americans.

Thanks to American intelligence the American warships evaded the Japanese submarine cordon and by June 1 were stationed 325 miles north-east of Midway.

Two days later the enemy was sighted by reconnaissance aircraft. A force of unescorted B-17 bombers were sent to attack the Japanese but without much success. The Japanese continued their approach towards the island. When 200 miles north of the island the bombers and fighter planes were sent in to destroy the local island force. The Americans spotted the strike and 15 Flying Fortresses were sent to attack the carriers while fighter planes rose to intercept the Japanese bombers. The inferior U.S. fighters were outnumbered and outclassed by the Japanese Zeros. Fifteen fighters were shot down and seven badly mauled. The Japanese bombers got

Yorktown *receives direct hit from Japanese assault plane.*

through and wreaked havoc on the completely defenceless island.

Later the same morning Admiral Nagumo gave orders for a second attack on Midway. But then he learnt of the presence of the American carrier force 200 miles to the east. Countermanding his previous order he gave directions for an assault on the American ships. Meanwhile American dive-bombers from Midway maintained a steady harassment of the Japanese.

By 9.00 a.m. all the Japanese carrier planes which had gone out on the Midway strike were recovered and Nagumo turned his ships north, preparing to do battle with the American carriers.

At 9.20, with his flight deck still clogged with planes, Nagumo was informed of the approach of enemy aircraft. The American carrier force was about to strike.

Sixty-eight dive-bombers, 29 torpedo planes and 24 Wildcat fighters from the *Enterprise* and *Hornet* rushed to engage the enemy. A little while later Fletcher, on the *Yorktown*, ordered

17 dive bombers, 12 torpedo planes and six fighters to join in the attack. The *Hornet* strike force arrived at the reported enemy position only to find nothing there. Nagumo had evaded the attack group by moving north. The initial carrier attack proved a disastrous failure. Of 41 torpedo planes only four survived and none of the torpedoes found their mark. Yet the suicidal torpedo attack paved the way for an American victory. Arriving late on the scene of battle, 33 dive-bombers from the *Enterprise* had an unopposed run on the four Japanese aircraft carriers. Bomb after bomb hit into the *Akagi* and *Kaga*. The *Enterprise* force was soon joined by the *Yorktown* bombers, who immediately took on the *Soryu*. The American bombs did their deadly work, leaving only the *Hiryu* undamaged. The Japanese immediately launched a counter attack, badly damaging the *Yorktown* but losing three fighters and thirteen dive bombers. A second attack was ordered in the early afternoon which led to the abandonment of the *Yorktown*. But by late afternoon the *Hiryu* had been spotted by the Americans, who launched a strike force of fourteen dive-bombers against the Japanese carrier, which was finally knocked out. The Americans won the battle, a victory almost solely due to the power of her aircraft carriers.

As the war progressed the carrier played an ever more vital role in defeating the Japanese.

A water-colour painted from memory by Lt. D. C. Chepler of a kamikaze attack on the USS Hornet.

The Super-carriers: a self-contained Island

The end of the Second World War left the Americans as the strongest naval power in the world. Post-war developments saw a continued emphasis on aircraft carriers. Three new battle carriers were completed between 1945 and 1947.

Known as the Midway carriers, they included for the first time an armoured flight deck in the design. They were enormous ships measuring 968 feet in length and 113 feet across. Armed with 16 five-inch guns, 84 40-mm and 28 20-mm anti-aircraft guns. the new carriers could support 123 aircraft and maintain a steady, impressive speed of 33 knots.

The introduction of jet-propelled aircraft forced further rethinking of carrier design. The faster, heavier planes required more powerful launching systems and longer landing runs. In 1951 the British operated the first steam-driven catapult. This was infinitely more powerful than previous ones.

Previously the flight deck was divided into two parts; the forward third was used as an aircraft park while the remaining two-thirds, separated by a crash barrier, formed the landing and launching area. It was suggested that by angling the landing area the crash barrier could be dispensed with and planes failing to pick up the landing wire could fly on and circle to make another attempt. Initial trials on H.M.S. *Triumph* and U.S.S. *Midway* were so successful that an elongated landing deck was immediately built into the U.S.S. *Antietnam*, jutting out over the port side.

The canted flight deck and the steam catapult were employed in succeeding carriers of all navies, including the American 'super-carrier', the *Enterprise*, completed in 1961.

Displacing 74,700 tons, she is 1,123 feet long. She has an angled flight deck, four steam catapults, four elevators, and a large starboard island structure.

From the front the island structure resembles a large billboard, being completely square except for a large central dome-shaped structure covered with fixed-array radar antennae and other electronic equipment.

The *Enterprise* is driven by eight nuclear reactors supplying to eight turbines which turn four screws. The ship's original nuclear 'core' enabled her to steam for three years, covering 200,000 miles before refuelling. The replacement core enabled the mileage, impressive as it was, to be increased by 25 per cent.

The development of nuclear weapons foreshadows the eventual decline of the aircraft carrier. The aircraft carrier is not as powerful a deterrent as the nuclear submarine and is more vulnerable to attack. It seems that it will more and more drift into an auxiliary role, its functions being taken over by the guided missile. In the Vietnam War the carrier was used mainly as a support vessel for land engagements.

Far left: HMS Ark Royal *modernised in 1970 to operate the Phantom II fighter. Left: The nuclear powered* USS Enterprise. *An enormously versatile ship, she can carry up to a hundred aircraft, including fighter aircraft for defence, strike aircraft, bombers and helicopters. The photo shows a view of the 'island' on the flight deck with its mass of antennae and radar equipment. Right: The flight deck of the* Enterprise — *1040 ft long and 257 ft wide.*

An unusual characteristic of the United States Navy's acoustic-homing torpedo, MK 32 — it does not have to be fired from a torpedo tube but can be tossed over the side of the ship from an open launcher. Below: Long Beach, the United States' first nuclear powered surface ship a guided missile cruiser. Opposite top: The U.S. guided missile cruiser Albany fires three surface-to-air missiles simultaneously.

Opposite below: One of Britain's latest nuclear-powered submarines armed with atomic missiles — the Navy's deadliest weapon.

NUCLEAR POWER – WEAPONS FOR THE FUTURE

After the Second World War the only major development in battleships was the introduction of the nuclear-powered turbine, the rocket and the nuclear-guided missiles.

The flying bomb was first successfully exploited by the Germans in their V1 and V2 rockets and later by the Japanese with their rocket-propelled Baka bomb. In response to the Baka bomb the United States worked on an interceptor missile. For this they employed the ram-jet to give it supersonic speed.

The ram-jet dispenses with the bulk and weight of the turbine and air compressor of the turbo jet. It uses compressed air pushed into the front end by the forward motion of the missile. The air is then mixed with kerosene to burn and expand. The hot air is pushed out through the nozzle by the inflowing air, thus providing the jet power. Its major drawback is that an initial forward thrust is needed. That problem was solved by using a booster-jet to launch the missile. A radar guidance system was fitted to the ram-jet missile (called the Terrier) and made its first fully-guided flight in 1948. The Terrier had a range of just over ten miles, which at twice the speed of sound and operating at a maximum altitude of 50,000 feet can intercept planes moving at 600 miles per hour.

The cruisers U.S.S. *Canberra* and U.S.S. *Boston* were fitted with the new missiles in the early fifties. They retained some of their eight-inch guns and 40-mm anti-aircraft guns but most of the armament was removed to make room for the two missile launchers.

The launchers were loaded by being turned to a vertical position with the missile rising through the open deck hatches and engaging lugs fitted onto the launcher. The cruisers held 144 missiles

The world's first atomic-powered submarine, the Nautilus, *on her first test run (1955).*

stored below deck on a circular rotating wheel. This arrangement allowed a rate of fire of two missiles every thirty seconds.

The Talos nuclear warhead missiles driven by ram-jet were introduced soon after into the cruisers *Galverston*, *Little Rock* and *Oklahoma City*. Later the *Albany*, *Columbus* and *Chicago* were converted to complete nuclear armament without any standard ordnance.

The most advanced American missile cruiser built was the *Long Beach*. She was the first surface ship to be powered by nuclear-driven turbines. She also has the distinction of being the only American cruiser built after the Second World War. Completed in 1961, she is 721·5 feet long with a displacement of 14,200 tons. She is armed with two twin Terrier launchers forward and one twin Talos launcher aft. She also carries two eight-inch guns installed amidships (an afterthought). Though she was designed to carry eight Polaris missiles they were never installed.

The anti-submarine rocket (ASROC) was developed soon after the Terrier and Talos missiles. Signals of nearby submarines are fed into the ship's computer, which plots the exact position of the submarine and the course the torpedoes will take.

When fired from the deck of a ship the ASROC follows a ballistic trajectory and, upon hitting the water, the torpedo separates from the rocket. The torpedo's entry is slowed down by a parachute and on contact with salt water the torpedo's batteries are activated. It then begins a systematic sonic search for the submarine.

Another method of torpedo delivery was code named DASH. A radio-controlled, unmanned helicopter carries the torpedo to the area in which a submarine has been detected.

Polaris missile launched from the nuclear sub, George Washington *(1960).*

First officially released photo of SUBROC, a submarine launched anti-sub missile.

INDEX

ACKNOWLEDGEMENTS

The publishers would like to thank the following organizations and individuals for their kind permission to reproduce the pictures in this book:

Cooper-Bridgeman Library
50/51

Crown Copyright permission of the Controller, H.M.S.O.
Cover, 6/7 and 135

Mary Evans Picture Library
11, 18, 21 (top right and centre right), 30, 37 (top left), 38, 39, 58 (centre right), 64/65, 64 (centre), 65 (top and centre), 67, 68, 69 (top left), 72, 72/73, 78, 79, 80 (top right and centre left), 81 (bottom), 82 (centre left and bottom left), 88 (centre right and bottom), 88, 89 (top), 89, 102, 102/103, 104/105, 105

Michael Holford
15, 54, 114/115 (Courtesy Ministry of Defence)

Illustrated London News
69 (bottom right), 76/77, 80/81, 92/93, 101, 110 (bottom left), 122/123, 124/125, 129 (centre left)

Illustrated Newspapers Group
129 (centre right)

Imperial War Museum, London
8 (top and bottom), 84/85, 86, 94/95, 97, 99, 100, 108 (top right and centre right), 110 (top right and centre right), 128 (centre), 129 (top left)

Keystone
130, 132 (bottom right), 133, 134 (bottom)

Mansell Collection
20/21, 37 (top right), 64/65 (bottom), 81 (centre left)

National Maritime Museum
Cover and 34/35, 42/43, endpapers and 46, 47 (bottom right), 66/67

Popperfoto
87 (bottom), 98/99, 98, 113 (top left and bottom), 126/127 (top), 128 (top), 131, 134 (top left), 135 (top), 136/137 (bottom left and bottom right)

Science Museum, London
12, 22, 43 (centre), 49, 58 (centre left), 59, 60/61, 69 (bottom left), 82 (top left), 87 (top), 88/89 (centre), 120/121, 132 (bottom left)

Artists
Bill Robertshaw and George Tuckwell